THE COMPLETE MEDITERRANEAN DIET UK FOR BEGINNERS (FULL COLOUR PICTURES)

1000 Days Of Healthy And Affordable Recipes To Fall In Love With Home-Cooked Meals, Exercise, And Healthy Habits.

ELLA R. LOPEZ

Copyright© 2023 By Ella R. Lopez Rights Reserved

This book is copyright protected. It is only for personal use. You cannot amend, distribute, sell, use, quote or paraphrase any part of the content within this book, without the consent of the author or publisher.

Under no circumstances will any blame or legal responsibility be held against the publisher, or author, for any damages, reparation, or monetary loss due to the information contained within this book, either directly or indirectly.

Disclaimer Notice:

Please note the information contained within this document is for educational and entertainment purposes only. All effort has been executed to present accurate, up to date, reliable, complete information. No warranties of any kind are declared or implied. Readers acknowledge that the author is not engaged in the rendering of legal, financial, medical or professional advice. The content within this book has been derived from various sources. Please consult a licensed professional before attempting any techniques outlined in this book.

By reading this document, the reader agrees that under no circumstances is the author responsible for any losses, direct or indirect, that are incurred as a result of the use of the information contained within this document, including, but not limited to, errors, omissions, or inaccuracies.

Table of Contents

Introduction	1
Chapter 1	
Overview of the Mediterranean Diet	2
What is the Mediterranean Diet?	3
Focuses mostly on eating a delicious variety of plant-based foods.	3
Focus on high-fiber whole grains and healthy fats.	3
Why the Mediterranean Diet	3
Reduces The Risk of Heart Disease	3
Lowers the risk of and aids in managing diabetes	4
Improves Brain Health and Cognitive Function	4
Basic Tenets of the Mediterranean Lifestyle	4
Change your thoughts around meat	4
Enjoy Healthy Fats	5
Drink Red Wine	5
Chapter 2	
Your Mediterranean Kitchen	6
Stock Up on the Staples	7
Whole or cracked grains	7
Pasta	7
Lentils (brown, green, red)	8
Pantry Essentials	8
Olive oil	8
Nuts and seeds	8
Herbs and spices	8
Refrigerated and Frozen Essentials	9
Fish and seafood	9
Feta Cheese	9
Greek Yogurt	9
Chapter 3	
4-Week Meal Plan	10
Week 1	11
Week 2	11
Week 3	12
Week 4	12
Chapter 4	
Breakfast	13
Garlic & Bell Pepper Frittata	14
Caprese Scrambled Eggs	14
Italian Ricotta & Tomato Omelet	15
Eggs with Spinach & Nuts	15
Spicy Poached Eggs with Mushrooms	16
Spinach Frittata	16
Italian Frittata	17
Breakfast Polenta	17
Baked Ricotta with Pears	18
South of the Coast Sweet Potato Toast	18
Zummo Meso Mini Frittatas	19
Baklava Hot Porridge	19
Lemon–Olive Oil Breakfast Cakes with Berry Syrup	20
Breakfast Pita	20
Savory Sweet Potato Hash	21
Individual Baked Egg Casseroles	21
Overnight Pomegranate Muesli	21
Chapter 5	
Snacks & Side Dishes	22
Asparagus Frittata	23
Cheesy Chicken Omelet	23
Crunchy Orange-Thyme Chickpeas	24
Sesame-Thyme Mano'ushe Flatbread	24
Quick Garlic Mushrooms	25
Cheesy Dates	25
Mediterranean Trail Mix	26
Savory Mediterranean Popcorn	26
Olive Tapenade with Anchovies	27
Greek Deviled Eggs	27
Homemade Sea Salt Pita Chips	28
Greek Potato Skins with Olives and Feta	28
Arabil--Style Spiced Roasted Chickpeas	29
Apple Chips With Chocolate Tahini	29
Strawberry Caprese Skewers	30
Rocket Salad with Figs, Prosciutto, Walnuts, and Parmesan	30
Rocket Salad with Pear, Almonds, Goat Cheese, and Apricots	30
Chapter 6	
Chicken and Poultry	31
Italian Chicken Thighs with Mushrooms	32
Chicken in Orange Gravy	32

Turkey with Rigatoni	32
Greek Turkey Meatballs	32
Chicken with Salsa Verde	33
Chicken with Mixed Vegetables	33
Greek Chicken Meatballs	33
Roasted Red Pepper Chicken with Lemony Garlic Hummus	33
Tahini Chicken Rice Bowls	34
Garlic-Lemon Chicken and Potatoes	34
Whole-Roasted Spanish Chicken	34
Lemon-Pepper Chicken Thighs	34
Sweet and Savory Stuffed Chicken	35
Spicy Turkey Meatballs	35
Spinach and Feta Stuffed Chicken	35
One-Pan Harissa Chicken and Brussels Sprouts with Yogurt Sauce	36
Chicken Piccata with Mushrooms	36
Bruschetta Chicken Burgers	36

Chapter 7
Beef, Lamb and Pork — 37

Jalapeño Pork	38
Dinner Pork Roast	38
Basil-Flavored Pork Stew	38
Beef & Vegetable Stew	38
Meatballs with Marinara Sauce	38
Italian-Style Pot Roast	39
Grilled Steak, Mushroom, and Onion Kebabs	39
Smoky Herb Lamb Cutlets and Lemon-Rosemary Dressing	39
Beef Kebabs with Tahini Sauce	40
Seasoned Beef Kebabs	40
Garlic Pork Fillet and Lemony Orzo	41
Roasted Pork with Apple-Dijon Sauce	41
Skirt steak with Orange-Herb Pistou	42
One-Pan Creamy Italian Bangers Orecchiette	42
Stuffed Pork Loin with Sun-Dried Tomato and Goat Cheese	43
Pork Fillet With Chermoula Sauce	43
Grilled Filet Mignon With Red Wine–Mushroom Sauce	44
Greek-Style Braised Pork with Leeks	44

Chapter 8
Fish and Seafood — 45

Prawn & Clam Paella	46
Haddock Fillets with Crushed Potatoes	46
Seafood Spicy Penne	46
Prawn Farfalle with Spinach	46
Mussel Chowder with Oyster Water biscuits	47
Baked Swordfish with Herbs	47
Garlic Rosemary Prawns	47
Air-Fried Crumbed Fish	47
Parmesan Garlic Crusted Salmon	47
Sicilian Kale and Tunny Bowl	48
Mediterranean Cod Stew	48
Grilled Sea Bass with Tahini Sauce	49
Spicy Trout over Sautéed Mediterranean Salad	49
Rosemary and Lemon Roasted Branzino	50
Tunny Slow-Cooked in Olive Oil	50
Prawn Ceviche Salad	51
Lemon-Pepper Trout	51

Chapter 9
Vegetarian Recipes — 52

Rocket Pizza	53
Aubergine Lasagna	53
Spinach and Leeks with Goat Cheese	53
Colorful Vegetable Medley	53
Roasted Brussels Sprouts with Orange and Garlic	53
Sweet Chickpea & Mushroom Stew	54
Asparagus and Prosciutto	54
Balsamic Cabbage	54
Citrus Asparagus with Pistachios	54
Gorgonzola Sweet Potato Burgers	54
Courgette-Aubergine Gratin	55
Roasted Cauliflower and Tomatoes	55
Roasted Acorn Squash	55
Quick Vegetable Kebabs	56
Tortellini in Red Pepper Sauce	56
Moroccan Vegetable Tagine	56
Parmesan and Herb Sweet Potatoes	56

Chapter 10
Desserts — 57

Honey Crema Catalana	58
Marble Cherry Cake	58
Simple Apricot Dessert	58
Dried Fruit Compote	58
Stewed Plums with Almond Flakes	59
Turkish Stuffed Apricots with Rose Water and Pistachios	59
Pomegranate-Quinoa Dark Chocolate Bark	59
Mini Mixed Berry Crumbles	59
Crunchy Sesame Scones	60
Almond Scones	60
Citrus Pound Cake	60
Individual Apple Pockets	60
Strawberry Panna Cotta	61
Chocolate Chia Pudding	61
Olive Oil Cake	61
Grilled Fruit Kebabs With Honey Labneh	61

Appendix 1 Measurement Conversion Chart — 62
Appendix 2 The Dirty Dozen and Clean Fifteen — 63
Appendix 3 Index — 64

Introduction

The Mediterranean Diet is a dietary pattern that is based on the traditional foods consumed by the people of the Mediterranean region, particularly those of Greece, southern Italy, and Spain, in the mid-20th century.

IT IS CHARACTERIZED BY:

- An emphasis on plant-based foods, such as fruits, vegetables, whole grains, legumes, and nuts.
- The use of olive oil as the primary source of fat.
- A moderate consumption of dairy products, poultry, and eggs.
- A low consumption of red meat and processed foods.
- A moderate consumption of wine, typically with meals.

Chapter 1
Overview of the Mediterranean Diet

What is the Mediterranean Diet?

The Mediterranean Diet has been associated with a variety of health benefits, including a lower risk of heart disease, stroke, and certain cancers. It is considered a healthy and sustainable way of eating that is based on whole, nutrient-dense foods and balanced meal patterns.

Focuses mostly on eating a delicious variety of plant-based foods.

The Mediterranean Diet places a strong emphasis on plant-based foods, such as fruits, vegetables, whole grains, legumes, and nuts, which are rich in essential nutrients, fiber, and healthy fats. These foods form the foundation of the diet and make up a large portion of each meal.

In addition to plant-based foods, the Mediterranean Diet also includes moderate amounts of dairy products, poultry, eggs, and fish, as well as a limited amount of red meat and processed foods. The use of olive oil as the primary source of fat, rather than other types of oils or butter, is also a key characteristic of the diet.

By focusing on a variety of delicious and nutrient-dense plant-based foods, the Mediterranean Diet provides a sustainable and healthy approach to eating that can promote overall health and well-being.

Focus on high-fiber whole grains and healthy fats.

The Mediterranean Diet places a strong emphasis on whole, fiber-rich grains and healthy fats.

Whole grains, such as brown rice, whole wheat, barley, and quinoa, are an important part of the Mediterranean Diet. They provide fiber, vitamins, minerals, and antioxidants, and help to promote satiety and maintain healthy blood sugar levels.

Healthy fats, particularly monounsaturated and polyunsaturated fats, are also a key component of the Mediterranean Diet. Olive oil is the primary source of fat in this dietary pattern, and it is used both for cooking and as a condiment. Nuts, seeds, and avocados are also good sources of healthy fats, and they provide additional benefits, such as protein and healthy oils.

Eating a diet that is rich in fiber-rich whole grains and healthy fats is associated with a range of health benefits, including improved heart health, weight management, and reduced risk of chronic diseases.

Why the Mediterranean Diet

Reduces The Risk of Heart Disease

The Mediterranean Diet has been shown to reduce the risk of heart disease through a number of mechanisms, including:

Decreased Inflammation: Inflammation is a major contributor to heart disease, and the Mediterranean Diet has been shown to reduce inflammation levels in the body. This is due to the high intake of anti-inflammatory foods, such as fruits, vegetables, whole grains, and healthy fats like olive oil.

Improved Cholesterol Levels: The Mediterranean Diet is low in unhealthy fats and high in monounsaturated fats like olive oil, which has been shown to improve cholesterol levels. Good cholesterol (HDL) levels are increased, while levels of bad cholesterol (LDL) are decreased.

Lower Blood Pressure: The Mediterranean Diet is high in potassium, magnesium, and fiber, which are all associated with lower blood pressure levels. A diet rich in these nutrients can help reduce the risk of high blood pressure, a major risk factor for heart disease.

Weight Management: The Mediterranean Diet encourages the consumption of fiber-rich foods, such as fruits, vegetables, and whole grains, which can help with weight management. Maintaining a healthy weight is important for reducing the risk of heart disease, as obesity is a major risk factor.

Physical Activity: The Mediterranean Diet encourages physical activity, which is important for maintaining heart health. Regular exercise helps to reduce the risk of heart disease by improving cardiovascular function and reducing the risk of obesity and other heart disease risk factors.

Lowers the risk of and aids in managing diabetes

The Mediterranean Diet has been shown to be effective in reducing the risk of developing type 2 diabetes and in managing the symptoms of those who already have the condition. Here are a few ways in which the Mediterranean Diet helps:

High fiber intake: The Mediterranean Diet is rich in fiber, which has been shown to help regulate blood sugar levels. This is particularly important for people with diabetes, who need to maintain stable blood sugar levels to manage their condition.

Low glycemic index: The Mediterranean Diet emphasizes foods with a low glycemic index, which means they are absorbed into the bloodstream more slowly and don't cause rapid spikes in blood sugar. This helps to prevent sudden increases in blood sugar, which can be particularly dangerous for people with diabetes.

Low glycemic load: The Mediterranean Diet also has a low glycemic load, meaning the total amount of carbohydrates consumed is relatively low, which helps to regulate blood sugar levels and reduces the risk of developing type 2 diabetes.

Healthy fats: The Mediterranean Diet emphasizes the consumption of healthy fats, such as olive oil, which have been shown to have a positive effect on insulin sensitivity, reducing the risk of developing type 2 diabetes.

Weight management: The Mediterranean Diet is associated with a healthy weight, which is important for people with diabetes. Maintaining a healthy weight can help to regulate blood sugar levels, improve insulin sensitivity, and reduce the risk of developing complications associated with diabetes.

Improves Brain Health and Cognitive Function

Studies have shown that following a Mediterranean Diet may have a positive impact on brain health and cognitive function. Here are a few ways this diet may help improve brain health:

Anti-inflammatory effect: A diet rich in fruits, vegetables, nuts, and whole grains that are found in the Mediterranean Diet can reduce inflammation in the body, which has been linked to a lower risk of cognitive decline and dementia.

Antioxidant effect: Antioxidants, such as those found in fruits, vegetables, and olive oil, protect the brain from damage caused by free radicals and oxidative stress.

Boosts blood flow: The Mediterranean Diet has been associated with improved blood flow to the brain, which is important for maintaining healthy brain function.

Promotes healthy aging: A diet that is rich in healthy fats and low in unhealthy fats may help protect against age-related cognitive decline. The Mediterranean Diet's emphasis on monounsaturated fats found in olive oil and omega-3 fatty acids found in fish may play a role in this protective effect.

Supports healthy gut microbiome: The Mediterranean Diet is also beneficial for the gut microbiome, which is increasingly recognized as playing an important role in cognitive function.

Basic Tenets of the Mediterranean Lifestyle

Change your thoughts around meat

When following the Mediterranean Diet, it's important to change your thoughts around meat. Rather than viewing meat as the main event in a meal, it should be used more as a flavoring or complement to dishes.

The Mediterranean Diet emphasizes plant-based foods, such as fruits, vegetables, whole grains, beans, and legumes, as the foundation of a healthy diet. Meat, including red meat, is consumed in smaller portions and is typically used to flavor dishes, rather than being the main feature.

By reducing the amount of meat in your diet and increasing the consumption of plant-based foods, you can reap the benefits of a diet that is low in unhealthy fats and high in fiber, antioxidants, and other nutrients that are important for overall health.

In addition, choosing lean cuts of meat, such as poultry and fish, and avoiding processed meats, can help reduce the risk of heart disease, type 2 diabetes, and other chronic health conditions.

Enjoy Healthy Fats

The Mediterranean Diet is known for its emphasis on healthy fats, particularly monounsaturated fats found in olive oil. These healthy fats have been shown to have a number of health benefits, including reducing inflammation, improving cholesterol levels, and promoting heart health.

In the Mediterranean Diet, olive oil is used as the primary source of fat in cooking and as a dressing for salads and vegetables. Nuts, seeds, and avocados are also included as sources of healthy fats.

It's important to note that while the Mediterranean Diet encourages the consumption of healthy fats, it still emphasizes moderation. Saturated and trans fats, which are unhealthy fats, should be limited. The goal is to balance the diet with a variety of healthy fats, proteins, and carbohydrates.

Drink Red Wine

Moderate red wine consumption is part of the traditional Mediterranean Diet, but it is not necessary for everyone who follows this diet to consume alcohol. The important thing is to follow a healthy and balanced eating pattern, with plenty of fruits, vegetables, whole grains, healthy fats, and lean proteins.

For those who choose to drink red wine, it is recommended to limit consumption to one to two glasses per day for men and one glass per day for women, as excessive alcohol intake has been linked to a range of health problems, including an increased risk of heart disease and certain types of cancer.

It is also important to remember that not everyone should drink alcohol, including pregnant women, individuals with liver disease, and those who are recovering from alcohol dependency.

The key to a healthy diet is to choose a variety of healthy foods and limit the consumption of foods that are high in unhealthy fats, sugar, and salt. Whether or not you choose to include red wine in your diet is a personal decision, but it is important to do so in moderation if you do decide to drink.

Chapter 2
Your Mediterranean Kitchen

Stock Up on the Staples

Whole or cracked grains

Whole or cracked grains are important staples to stock up in a Mediterranean diet kitchen because they provide fiber and nutrients that are important for overall health. Some of the whole or cracked grains that can be included in a Mediterranean diet include:

WHOLE WHEAT OR WHOLE GRAIN BREAD

Brown rice
Quinoa
Bulgur
Barley
Whole grain pasta
Oatmeal

These whole or cracked grains are a good source of carbohydrates, fiber, and essential vitamins and minerals, and they can help you feel full and satisfied for longer after a meal. Additionally, incorporating these grains into your meals can help you achieve a more balanced and healthy diet, which is a key aspect of the Mediterranean Diet.

Pasta

Whole grain pasta is a staple ingredient that can be found in many Mediterranean Diet kitchens. Unlike refined pasta made from white flour, whole grain pasta is a good source of fiber, vitamins, and minerals. It also has a lower glycemic index, which means it is absorbed more slowly into the bloodstream and can help regulate blood sugar levels.

In a Mediterranean Diet, pasta is often served as a complement to other dishes rather than the main course. It can be paired with vegetables, legumes, or a light sauce made with olive oil, herbs, and spices to create a balanced meal. Keeping whole grain pasta in the pantry allows you to have a quick and easy meal option when you are short on time or need a convenient lunch or dinner solution.

Lentils (brown, green, red)

lentils are an important staple in the Mediterranean Diet. They are a good source of plant-based protein, fiber, and various vitamins and minerals. Lentils can be used in a variety of dishes, such as soups, stews, salads, and side dishes. You can stock up on brown, green, or red lentils, and they can be easily stored in your pantry for long periods of time. Incorporating lentils into your meals is an easy way to add nutrition and variety to your diet.

Pantry Essentials

Olive oil

Olive oil is a staple ingredient in the Mediterranean Diet, and it is recommended to stock up on this ingredient when following this dietary approach. Olive oil is a good source of monounsaturated fats, which have been shown to help reduce the risk of heart disease and improve overall health. In a Mediterranean Diet, olive oil is used in place of other fats, such as butter or margarine, and it is used to flavor dishes, dress salads, and to cook with. When purchasing olive oil, it is recommended to look for extra-virgin olive oil, which is the least processed form of olive oil and has the highest level of heart-healthy monounsaturated fats.

Nuts and seeds

Nuts and seeds are an important part of the Mediterranean Diet and should be stocked up in a Mediterranean diet kitchen. Some of the nuts and seeds that can be included in a Mediterranean diet include:

Almonds: Almonds are a good source of healthy fats, protein, and fiber, and they can be eaten raw, roasted, or as almond butter.

Walnuts: Walnuts are a good source of healthy fats and antioxidants, and they can be added to salads, yogurt, or baked goods.

Pistachios: Pistachios are a good source of healthy fats and protein, and they can be eaten as a snack or added to dishes as a garnish.

Hazelnuts: Hazelnuts are a good source of healthy fats and fiber, and they can be used to make nut butter or added to baked goods.

Sesame seeds: Sesame seeds are a good source of healthy fats and minerals, and they can be added to dishes as a garnish or used to make tahini.

Having a variety of nuts and seeds on hand can help you add flavor and nutrition to a variety of dishes, making it easy to follow a Mediterranean diet.

Herbs and spices

Herbs and spices are an important part of the Mediterranean Diet and they can help add flavor to dishes while reducing the need for added salt and sugar. Some of the herbs and spices that you may want to stock up on in a Mediterranean Diet kitchen include:

Basil: A fragrant herb that is commonly used in Mediterranean dishes, such as pesto and tomato sauce.

Oregano: A strong, savory herb that is commonly used in Mediterranean dishes, such as roasted vegetables and pizza.

Rosemary: A fragrant herb with a pine-like flavor, rosemary is commonly used in Mediterranean dishes, such as roasted potatoes and chicken.

Thyme: A delicate, minty herb that is commonly used in Mediterranean dishes, such as stews and soups.

Garlic: A pungent bulb used for flavor in many Mediterranean dishes.

Paprika: A mild to medium-hot spice made from dried red peppers that is used for flavor and color in Mediterranean dishes.

Cumin: A warm and slightly bitter spice that is used in Mediterranean dishes, such as soups and stews.

Coriander: A citrusy and slightly sweet spice that is used in Mediterranean dishes, such as couscous and hummus.

Having these herbs and spices on hand can help you add flavor to your meals, and they can also help you create quick and healthy meals without having to make a trip to the grocery store.

Refrigerated and Frozen Essentials

Fish and seafood

In a Mediterranean Diet kitchen, it is recommended to stock up on refrigerated and frozen fish and seafood, as they are a key source of protein and healthy fats. Some popular options include salmon, sardines, anchovies, and mussels.

Refrigerated fish and seafood can be a convenient option for quick meals, as they can be easily cooked in a variety of ways, such as grilling, roasting, or pan-frying. Frozen seafood can also be a good option, as it can be stored for a longer period of time and used when needed.

It is important to choose fish and seafood that are high in omega-3 fatty acids, which have been shown to have numerous health benefits, including reducing the risk of heart disease, improving brain function, and reducing inflammation.

Incorporating fish and seafood into your diet on a regular basis is an easy way to follow the principles of the Mediterranean Diet, and can help ensure that you are getting the nutrients you need for overall health and wellness.

Feta Cheese

Feta cheese is a staple ingredient in the Mediterranean Diet. It is a tangy, crumbly cheese that is commonly used in Mediterranean dishes, such as salads, dips, and pies. Feta is a good source of calcium, protein, and healthy fats, and it is lower in fat and calories compared to other types of cheese. When following a Mediterranean Diet, it is recommended to choose high-quality, authentic feta cheese, which is made from sheep's milk or a combination of sheep's and goat's milk. Stocking up on feta cheese in your kitchen can help you add flavor and variety to your meals and snacks.

Greek Yogurt

Greek yogurt can be a good ingredient to stock up in a Mediterranean Diet kitchen. Greek yogurt is a good source of protein and calcium, and it can be used in a variety of dishes, such as smoothies, dips, and sauces. It can also be a healthy alternative to high-fat dairy products, such as sour cream and mayonnaise, as it is lower in fat and calories. Additionally, Greek yogurt contains probiotics, which are beneficial bacteria that can help support digestive health. When stocking up on Greek yogurt, look for varieties that are low in sugar and made with natural ingredients.

Chapter 3
4-Week Meal Plan

Week 1

Here is the following first week's meal plan for the Mediterranean diet. Try to follow the plan thoroughly to start getting the benefits of a Mediterranean diet.

Meal Plan	Breakfast	Lunch	Dinner	Snack
Day-1	Caprese Scrambled Eggs	Chicken in Orange Gravy	Prawn & Clam Paella	Honey Crema Catalana
Day-2	Caprese Scrambled Eggs	Mediterranean Cod Stew	Dinner Pork Roast	Honey Crema Catalana
Day-3	Eggs with Spinach & Nuts	Air-Fried Crumbed Fish	Chicken with Salsa Verde	Honey Crema Catalana
Day-4	Spinach Frittata	Beef & Vegetable Stew	Prawn Ceviche Salad	Marble Cherry Cake
Day-5	Breakfast Polenta	Mediterranean Cod Stew	Mediterranean Cod Stew	Marble Cherry Cake
Day-6	Italian Frittata	Prawn & Clam Paella	Chicken in Orange Gravy	Marble Cherry Cake
Day-7	Breakfast Polenta	Greek Chicken Meatballs	Dinner Pork Roast	Marble Cherry Cake

Week 2

Here is the following second week's meal plan for a Mediterranean diet. It's the second stage of the 4 weeks meal plan that you must take into account carefully.

Meal Plan	Breakfast	Lunch	Dinner	Snack
Day-1	Caprese Scrambled Eggs	Italian-Style Pot Roast	Aubergine Lasagna	Simple Apricot Dessert
Day-2	Italian Frittata	Seafood Spicy Penne	Chicken in Orange Gravy	Simple Apricot Dessert
Day-3	Eggs with Spinach & Nuts	Mediterranean Cod Stew	Prawn Farfalle with Spinach	Simple Apricot Dessert
Day-4	Breakfast Polenta	Prawn Ceviche Salad	Tahini Chicken Rice Bowls	Simple Apricot Dessert
Day-5	Breakfast Polenta	Aubergine Lasagna	Dinner Pork Roast	Dried Fruit Compote
Day-6	Baked Ricotta with Pears	Air-Fried Crumbed Fish	Turkey with Rigatoni	Dried Fruit Compote
Day-7	Baked Ricotta with Pears	Italian-Style Pot Roast	Seafood Spicy Penne	Dried Fruit Compote

Week 3

Here is the following third week's meal plan for a Mediterranean diet. In this stage, you already got the result of the previous two weeks' diet plan. So, follow this third stage of the meal plan completely to get a better result.

Meal Plan	Breakfast	Lunch	Dinner	Snack
Day-1	Eggs with Spinach & Nuts	Greek Turkey Meatballs	Colorful Vegetable Medley	Crunchy Sesame Scones
Day-2	Breakfast Polenta	Balsamic Cabbage	Basil-Flavored Pork Stew	Crunchy Sesame Scones
Day-3	Caprese Scrambled Eggs	Prawn Ceviche Salad	Turkey with Rigatoni	Crunchy Sesame Scones
Day-4	Baked Ricotta with Pears	Roasted Acorn Squash	Prawn Farfalle with Spinach	Almond Scones
Day-5	Italian Frittata	Tahini Chicken Rice Bowls	Roasted Acorn Squash	Almond Scones
Day-6	Zummo Meso Mini Frittata	Balsamic Cabbage	Turkey with Rigatoni	Almond Scones
Day-7	Baked Ricotta with Pears	Basil-Flavored Pork Stew	Garlic Rosemary Prawns	Almond Scones

Week 4

This is the final stage of our 4 week's Mediterranean diet meal plan. In this stage, you already have formed a habit of maintaining a Mediterranean diet. So, follow this final stage to get best the best result in your body and mind.

Meal Plan	Breakfast	Lunch	Dinner	Snack
Day-1	Italian Frittata	Spicy Turkey Meatballs	Lemon-Pepper Trout	Citrus Pound Cake
Day-2	Baked Ricotta with Pears	Colorful Vegetable Medley	Greek Turkey Meatballs	Citrus Pound Cake
Day-3	Zummo Meso Mini Frittatas	Chicken with Salsa Verde	Garlic Rosemary Prawns	Citrus Pound Cake
Day-4	Italian Frittata	Asparagus and Prosciutto	Seasoned Beef Kebabs	Individual Apple Pockets
Day-5	Individual Baked Egg Casseroles	Prawn Ceviche Salad	Whole-Roasted Spanish Chicken	Individual Apple Pockets
Day-6	Individual Baked Egg Casseroles	Beef & Vegetable Stew	Seasoned Beef Kebabs	Individual Apple Pockets
Day-7	Individual Baked Egg Casseroles	Lemon-Pepper Trout	Greek Turkey Meatballs	Individual Apple Pockets

Chapter 4
Breakfast

Garlic & Bell Pepper Frittata

Prep time: 10 minutes|Cook time:10 minutes|Serves 2

- 2 red capsicums, chopped
- 4 eggs
- 2 tbsp olive oil
- 2 garlic cloves, crushed
- 1 tsp Italian Seasoning mix

1. Grease the pot with oil.
2. Stir-fry the peppers for 2-3 minutes, or until lightly charred.
3. Set aside. Add garlic and stir-fry for 1 minute, until soft.
4. Whisk the eggs and season with Italian seasoning.
5. Pour the mixture into the pot and cook for 2-3 minutes, or until set.
6. Using a spatula, loosen the edges and gently slide onto a plate.
7. Add charred peppers and fold over.
8. Serve hot.

Caprese Scrambled Eggs

Prep time: 5 minutes|Cook time:20 minutes|Serves 5

- 4 eggs
- ½ cup fresh mozzarella cheese
- 1 cup button mushrooms, chopped
- 1 large tomato, chopped
- 2 spring onions, chopped
- ¼ cup milk
- 2 tbsp olive oil
- ½ tsp salt

1. Grease the pot with oil and set on Sauté.
2. Stir-fry the onions for 3 minutes, or until translucent.
3. Add tomatoes and mushrooms.
4. Cook until liquid evaporates, for 5-6 minutes.
5. Meanwhile, Whisk eggs, cheese, milk, and salt.
6. Pour into the pot and stir.
7. Cook for 2 minutes, or until set.

Italian Ricotta & Tomato Omelet
Prep time: 5 minutes|Cook time: 25 minutes|Serves 4

- 1 lb tomatoes, peeled, roughly diced
- 1 tbsp tomato paste
- 1 tsp brown sugar
- 1 cup ricotta cheese
- 4 eggs
- 3 tbsp olive oil
- 1 tbsp Italian seasoning mix
- ¼ cup fresh parsley, chopped
- ¼ tsp salt

1. Grease the inner pot with oil.
2. Press Sauté and add tomatoes, sugar, Italian seasoning, parsley, and salt.
3. Give it a good stir and cook for 15 minutes or until the tomatoes soften.
4. Stir occasionally.
5. Meanwhile, whisk eggs and cheese.
6. Pour the mixture into the pot stir well.
7. Cook for 3 more minutes.
8. Serve immediately.

Eggs with Spinach & Nuts
Prep time: 5 minutes|Cook time: 20 minutes|Serves 4

- 1 lb spinach, rinsed, chopped
- 3 tbsp olive oil
- 1 tbsp butter
- 1 tbsp almonds, crushed
- 1 tbsp ground nuts, crushed
- 4 eggs
- ½ tsp Chili con carne flakes
- ½ tsp sea salt

1. Pour 1 ½ cups of water into the inner pot and insert a steamer basket.
2. Place the eggs onto the basket.
3. Seal the lid and cook on High Pressure for 5 minutes.
4. Do a quick release.
5. Remove the eggs to an ice bath.
6. Wipe the pot clean, and heat oil on Sauté.
7. Add spinach and cook for 2-3 minutes, stirring occasionally.
8. Stir in 1 tbsp of butter and season with salt and Chili con carne flakes.
9. Mix well and cook for 1 more minute.
10. Press Cancel and sprinkle with nuts.
11. Peel and rasher each egg in half, lengthwise.
12. Transfer to a serving plate and pour over spinach mixture.

Spicy Poached Eggs with Mushrooms

Prep time: 5 minutes|Cook time:20 minutes|Serves 1

- 3 oz button mushrooms, cut half lengthwise
- 2 oz fresh rocket
- 1 egg
- 2 tbsp olive oil
- Chili con carne flakes, for Seasoning

1. Melt butter on Sauté, add mushrooms and cook for 4-5 minutes, until soft. Stir in rocket.
2. Cook for one minute.
3. Crack the egg and cook until set – for 2 minutes.
4. Season with Chili con carne flakes.
5. Press Cancel and remove the omelet to a serving plate.

Spinach Frittata

Prep time: 5 minutes|Cook time:8 minutes|Serves 1

- Three eggs
- One cup spinach, chopped
- One small onion, minced
- 2 tbsp mozzarella cheese, grated
- Salt and Pepper

1. Preheat the Air Fryer to 125.
2. Spray a pan with cook spray.
3. In a bowl, whisk the eggs with the remaining ingredients until well combined.
4. Pour the egg mixture into the prepared pan and place it in the Air Fryer basket.
5. Cook frittata for eight mins.

Italian Frittata

Prep time: 5 minutes | Cook time: 10 minutes | Serves 6

- Six eggs
- 1/3 cup of milk
- 4-ounces of chopped Italian bangers
- Three cups of stemmed and roughly chopped kale
- One red deseeded and chopped bell pepper
- ½ cup of a grated feta cheese
- One chopped Courgette
- 1 tablespoon of freshly chopped basil
- 1 teaspoon of garlic powder
- 1 teaspoon of onion powder
- 1 teaspoon of salt
- 1 teaspoon of black pepper

1. Preheat the Air Fryer to 135 .
2. Grease a pan with a nonstick cook spray.
3. Add the Italian bangers to the pan and cook it in your Air Fryer for five minutes.
4. Add and toss in the remaining ingredients until it mixes properly.
5. Add the egg mixture and let it cook in your Air Fryer for five minutes.
6. After that, carefully remove the pan and let it cool before serving.

Breakfast Polenta

Prep time: 5 minutes | Cook time: 10 minutes | Serves 6

- 2 (18-ounce) tubes plain polenta
- 2¼ to 2½ cups 2% milk, divided
- 2 oranges, peeled and chopped
- ½ cup chopped pecans
- ¼ cup 2% plain Greek yogurt
- 8 teaspoons honey

1. Rasher the polenta into rounds and place in a microwave-safe bowl.
2. Heat in the microwave on high for 45 seconds.
3. Transfer the polenta to a large pot, and mash it with a potato masher or fork until coarsely mashed.
4. Place the pot on the stove over medium heat.
5. In a medium, microwave-safe bowl, heat the milk in the microwave on high for 1 minute.
6. Pour 2 cups of the warmed milk into the pot with the polenta, and stir with a whisk.
7. Continue to stir and mash with the whisk, adding the remaining milk a few tablespoons at a time, until the polenta is fairly smooth and heated through, about 5 minutes.
8. Remove from the stove.
9. Divide the polenta among four serving bowls.
10. Top each bowl with one-quarter of the oranges, 2 tablespoons of pecans, 1 tablespoon of yogurt, and 2 teaspoons of honey before serving.

Baked Ricotta with Pears

Prep time: 5 minutes|Cook time:25 minutes|Serves 4

- Nonstick cooking spray
- 1 (16-ounce) container whole-milk ricotta cheese
- 2 large eggs
- ¼ cup white whole-wheat flour or whole-wheat pastry flour
- 1 tablespoon sugar
- 1 teaspoon vanilla extract
- ¼ teaspoon ground nutmeg
- 1 pear, cored and diced
- 2 tablespoons water
- 1 tablespoon honey

1. Preheat the oven to 200 .
2. Spray four 6-ounce ramekins with nonstick cooking spray.
3. In a large bowl, beat together the ricotta, eggs, flour, sugar, vanilla, and nutmeg.
4. Spoon into the ramekins. Bake for 22 to 25 minutes, or until the ricotta is just about set.
5. Remove from the oven and cool slightly on racks.
6. While the ricotta is baking, in a small saucepan over medium heat, simmer the pear in the water for 10 minutes, until slightly softened.
7. Remove from the heat, and stir in the honey.
8. Serve the ricotta ramekins topped with the warmed pear.

South of the Coast Sweet Potato Toast

Prep time: 5 minutes|Cook time:15 minutes|Serves 4

- 2 plum tomatoes, halved
- 6 tablespoons extra-virgin olive oil, divided
- Salt
- Freshly ground black pepper
- 2 large sweet potatoes, rasherd lengthwise
- 1 cup fresh spinach
- 8 medium asparagus, trimmed
- 4 large cooked eggs or egg substitute (poached, scrambled, or fried)
- 1 cup rocket
- 4 tablespoons pesto
- 4 tablespoons shredded Asiago cheese

1. Preheat the oven to 220 .
2. On a baking tray, brush the plum tomato halves with 2 tablespoons of olive oil and season with salt and pepper.
3. Roast the tomatoes in the oven for approximately 15 minutes, then remove from the oven and allow to rest.
4. Put the sweet potato rashers on a separate baking tray and brush about 2 tablespoons of oil on each side and season with salt and pepper.
5. Bake the sweet potato rashers for about 15 minutes, flipping once after 5 to 7 minutes, until just tender.
6. Remove from the oven and set aside.
7. In a sauté pan or frying pan, heat the remaining 2 tablespoons of olive oil over medium heat and sauté the fresh spinach until just wilted.
8. Remove from the pan and rest on a paper-towel-lined dish.
9. In the same pan, add the asparagus and sauté, turning throughout. Transfer to a paper towel-lined dish.
10. Place the rashers of grilled sweet potato on serving plates and divide the spinach and asparagus evenly among the rashers.
11. Place a prepared egg on top of the spinach and asparagus.
12. Top this with ¼ cup of rocket .
13. Finish by drizzling with 1 tablespoon of pesto and sprinkle with 1 tablespoon of cheese.
14. Serve with 1 roasted plum tomato.

Zummo Meso Mini Frittatas

Prep time: 10 minutes | Cook time: 25 minutes | Serves 6

- Nonstick cooking spray, olive oil, or butter
- 1½ tablespoons extra-virgin olive oil
- ¼ cup chopped red potatoes (about 3 small)
- ¼ cup minced onions
- ¼ cup chopped red bell pepper
- ¼ cup asparagus, rashered lengthwise in half and chopped
- 4 large eggs
- 4 large egg whites
- ½ cup Skimmed milk
- Salt
- Freshly ground black pepper
- ½ cup shredded low-moisture, part-skim mozzarella cheese, divided

1. Preheat the oven to 120 . Using nonstick cooking spray, prepare a 12-count muffin pan.
2. In a medium sauté pan or frying pan, heat the oil over medium heat and sauté the potatoes and onions for about 4 minutes, until the potatoes are fork-tender.
3. Add the bell pepper and asparagus and sauté for about 4 minutes, until just tender. Transfer the contents of a pan onto a paper-towel-lined plate to cool.
4. In a bowl, whisk together the eggs, egg whites, and milk. Season with salt and pepper.
5. Once the vegetables are cooled to room temperature, add the vegetables and ¼ cup of mozzarella cheese.
6. Using a spoon or ladle, evenly distribute the contents of the bowl into the prepared muffin pan, filling the cups about halfway.
7. Sprinkle the remaining ¼ cup of cheese over the top of the cups.
8. Bake for 20 to 25 minutes, or until eggs reach an internal temperature of 75 or the center is solid.
9. Allow the mini frittatas to rest for 5 to 10 minutes before removing from muffin pan and serving.

Baklava Hot Porridge

Prep time: 5 minutes | Cook time: 5 minutes | Serves 2

- 2 cups Riced Cauliflower
- ¾ cup unsweetened almond, flax, or hemp milk
- 4 tablespoons extra-virgin olive oil, divided
- 2 teaspoons grated fresh orange peel (from ½ orange)
- ½ teaspoon ground cinnamon
- ½ teaspoon almond extract or vanilla extract
- ⅛ teaspoon salt
- 4 tablespoons chopped walnuts, divided
- 1 to 2 teaspoons liquid stevia, monk fruit, or other sweetener of choice (optional)

1. In medium saucepan, combine the riced cauliflower, almond milk, 2 tablespoons olive oil, grated orange peel, cinnamon, almond extract, and salt.
2. Stir to combine and bring just to a boil over medium-high heat, stirring constantly.
3. Remove from heat and stir in 2 tablespoons chopped walnuts and sweetener (if using).
4. Stir to combine.
5. Divide into bowls, topping each with 1 tablespoon of chopped walnuts and 1 tablespoon of the remaining olive oil.

Lemon Olive Oil Breakfast Cakes with Berry Syrup

Prep time: 5 minutes|Cook time:10 minutes|Serves 4

- For the Pancakes
- 1 cup almond flour
- 1 teaspoon baking powder
- ¼ teaspoon salt
- 6 tablespoon extra-virgin olive oil, divided
- 2 large eggs
- Zest and juice of 1 lemon
- ½ teaspoon almond or vanilla extract
- For the Berry Sauce
- 1 cup frozen mixed berries
- 1 tablespoon water or lemon juice, plus more if needed
- ½ teaspoon vanilla extract

TO MAKE THE PANCAKES

1. In a large bowl, combine the almond flour, baking powder, and salt and whisk to break up any clumps.
2. Add the 4 tablespoons olive oil, eggs, lemon zest and juice, and almond extract and whisk to combine well.
3. In a large frying pan, heat 1 tablespoon of olive oil and spoon about 2 tablespoons of batter for each of 4 pancakes.
4. Cook until bubbles begin to form, 4 to 5 minutes, and flip.
5. Cook another 2 to 3 minutes on second side.
6. Repeat with remaining 1 tablespoon olive oil and batter.

TO MAKE THE BERRY SAUCE

1. In a small saucepan, heat the frozen berries, water, and vanilla essenceover medium-high for 3 to 4 minutes, until bubbly, adding more water if mixture is too thick.
2. Using the back of a spoon or fork, mash the berries and whisk until smooth.

Breakfast Pita

Prep time: 5 minutes|Cook time:6 minutes|Serves 2

- 1 whole wheat pita
- 2 teaspoons olive oil
- ½ shallot, diced
- ¼ teaspoon garlic, minced
- 1 large egg
- ¼ teaspoon dried oregano
- ¼ teaspoon dried thyme
- ⅛ teaspoon salt
- 2 tablespoons shredded Parmesan cheese

1. Preheat the air fryer to 190 .
2. Brush the top of the pita with olive oil, then spread the diced shallot and minced garlic over the pita.
3. Crack the egg into a small bowl or ramekin, and season it with oregano, thyme, and salt.
4. Place the pita into the air fryer basket, and gently pour the egg onto the top of the pita. Sprinkle with cheese over the top.
5. Bake for 6 minutes.
6. Allow to cool for 5 minutes before cutting into pieces for serving.

Savory Sweet Potato Hash
Prep time: 15 minutes | Cook time: 18 minutes | Serves 6

- 2 medium sweet potatoes, peeled and cut into 1-inch cubes
- ½ green bell pepper, diced
- ½ red onion, diced
- 4 ounces baby bella mushrooms, diced
- 2 tablespoons olive oil
- 1 garlic clove, minced
- ½ teaspoon salt
- ½ teaspoon black pepper
- ½ tablespoon chopped fresh rosemary

1. Preheat the air fryer to 190 .
2. In a large bowl, toss all ingredients together until the vegetables are well coated and seasonings distributed.
3. Pour the vegetables into the air fryer basket, making sure they are in a single even layer. (If using a smaller air fryer, you may need to do this in two batches.)
4. Cook for 9 minutes, then toss or flip the vegetables. Cook for 9 minutes more.
5. Transfer to a serving bowl or individual plates and enjoy.

Individual Baked Egg Casseroles
Prep time: 10 minutes | Cook time: 30 minutes | Serves 4

- 1 rasher whole-grain bread
- 4 large eggs, beaten
- 3 tablespoons milk
- ¼ teaspoon salt
- ½ teaspoon onion powder
- ¼ teaspoon garlic powder
- Pinch freshly ground black pepper
- ¾ cup chopped vegetables (any kind you like—e.g., cherry tomatoes, mushrooms, spring onions, spinach, broccoli, etc.)

1. Heat the oven to 145 and set the rack to the middle position.
2. Oil two 8-ounce ramekins and place them on a baking tray.
3. Tear the bread into pieces and line each ramekin with ½ of a rasher.
4. Mix the eggs, milk, salt, onion powder, garlic powder, pepper, and vegetables in a medium bowl.
5. Pour half of the egg mixture into each ramekin.
6. Bake for 30 minutes, or until the eggs are set.

Overnight Pomegranate Muesli
Prep time: 10 minutes | Cook time: 30 minutes | Serves 2

- ½ cup gluten-free old-fashioned oats
- ¼ cup shelled pistachios
- 3 tablespoons pumpkin seeds
- 2 tablespoons chia seeds
- ¾ cup milk
- ½ cup plain Greek yogurt
- 2 to 3 teaspoons maple syrup (optional)
- ½ cup pomegranate arils

1. In a medium bowl, mix together the oats, pistachios, pumpkin seeds, chia seeds, milk, yogurt, and maple syrup, if using.
2. Divide the mixture between two 12-ounce mason jars or another type of container with a lid.
3. Top each with ¼ cup of pomegranate arils.
4. Cover each jar or container and store in the refrigerator overnight or up to 4 days.
5. Serve cold, with additional milk if desired.

Chapter 5
Snacks & Side Dishes

Asparagus Frittata

Prep time: 10 minutes | Cook time: 5 minutes | Serves 2

- 4 eggs, whisked
- 3 Tablespoons parmesan, grated
- 2 Tablespoons milk
- Salt and black pepper to the taste
- Ten asparagus tips, steamed
- Cooking spray

1. In a bowl, mix the eggs with the parmesan, butter, salt, and pepper, and whisk well.
2. Heat the Air Fryer to 200 and drizzle with cooking spray.
3. Add the asparagus, mix the eggs, toss a little, and cook for 5 minutes.

Cheesy Chicken Omelet

Prep time: 5 minutes | Cook time: 18 minutes | Serves 2

- Cooked Chicken Breast: half cup (diced) divided
- Four eggs
- Onion powder: 1/4 tsp, divided
- Salt: 1/2 tsp., divided
- Pepper: 1/4 tsp., divided
- Shredded cheese: 2 tbsp. divided
- Garlic powder: 1/4 tsp, divided

1. Take two ramekins and grease them with olive oil.
2. Add two eggs to each ramekin. Then, add cheese with seasoning.
3. Blend to combine.
4. Add 1/4 cup of cooked chicken on top.
5. Cook for 18 minutes in the Air Fryer at 120 .

Crunchy Orange-Thyme Chickpeas
Prep time: 5 minutes|Cook time: 20 minutes|Serves 4

- 1 (15-ounce) can chickpeas, drained and rinsed
- 2 teaspoons extra-virgin olive oil
- ¼ teaspoon dried thyme or ½ teaspoon chopped fresh thyme leaves
- ⅛ teaspoon kosher or sea salt
- Zest of ½ orange (about ½ teaspoon)

1. Preheat the oven to 220 .
2. Spread the chickpeas on a clean kitchen towel, and rub gently until dry.
3. Spread the chickpeas on a large, rimmed baking tray.
4. Drizzle with the oil, and sprinkle with the thyme and salt.
5. Using a Microplane or citrus zester, zest about half of the orange over the chickpeas.
6. Mix well using your hands.
7. Bake for 10 minutes, then open the oven door and, using an oven mitt, give the baking tray a quick shake. (Do not remove the sheet from the oven.) Bake for 10 minutes more.
8. Taste the chickpeas (carefully!).
9. If they are golden but you think they could be a bit crunchier, bake for 3 minutes more before serving.

Sesame-Thyme Mano'ushe Flatbread
Prep time: 5 minutes|Cook time: 10 minutes|Serves 6

- Nonstick cooking spray
- 1 (16-ounce) bag whole-wheat pizza dough or 3 (6-inch) whole-wheat pita breads
- 3 tablespoons dried thyme
- 3 tablespoons sesame seeds
- 3 tablespoons extra-virgin olive oil
- ¼ teaspoon kosher or sea salt

1. Preheat the oven to 220 .
2. Spray a large, rimmed baking tray with nonstick cooking spray.
3. Divide the dough into three equal balls.
4. On a floured surface, roll each dough ball with a rolling pin into a 6-inch circle.
5. Place all three dough circles (or pita breads) on the baking tray.
6. In a small bowl, whisk together the thyme, sesame seeds, oil, and salt.
7. With a pastry brush or spoon, brush the oil onto the three dough circles (or pita breads) until it's all used up.
8. Bake the dough circles for 10 minutes, or until the edges just start to brown and crisp and the oil is cooked into the dough.
9. If using pita rounds, bake them for only 5 minutes.
10. Remove the flatbreads from the oven, cut each circle in half, and serve.

Quick Garlic Mushrooms

Prep time: 10 minutes|Cook time:10 minutes|Serves 4 to 6

- 2 pounds cremini mushrooms, cleaned
- 3 tablespoons unsalted butter
- 2 tablespoons garlic, minced
- ½ teaspoon salt
- ½ teaspoon freshly ground black pepper

1. Cut each mushroom in half, stem to top, and put them into a bowl.
2. Preheat a large sauté pan or frying pan over medium heat.
3. Cook the butter and garlic in the pan for 2 minutes, stirring occasionally.
4. Add the mushrooms and salt to the pan and toss together with the garlic butter mixture.
5. Cook for 7 to 8 minutes, stirring every 2 minutes.
6. Remove the mushrooms from the pan and pour into a serving dish.
7. Top with black pepper.

Cheesy Dates

Prep time: 15 minutes|Cook time:10 minutes|Serves 12 to 15

- 1 cup pecans, shells removed
- 1 (8-ounce) container mascarpone cheese
- 20 medjool dates

1. Preheat the oven to 170 .
2. Put the pecans on a baking tray and bake for 5 to 6 minutes, until lightly toasted and aromatic.
3. Take the pecans out of the oven and let cool for 5 minutes.
4. Once cooled, put the pecans in a food processor fitted with a chopping blade and chop until they resemble the texture of bulgur wheat or coarse sugar.
5. Reserve ¼ cup of ground pecans in a small bowl.
6. Pour the remaining chopped pecans into a larger bowl and add the mascarpone cheese.
7. Using a spatula, mix the cheese with the pecans until evenly combined.
8. Spoon the cheese mixture into a piping bag.
9. Using a knife, cut one side of the date lengthwise, from the stem to the bottom.
10. Gently open and remove the pit.
11. Using the piping bag, squeeze a generous amount of the cheese mixture into the date where the pit used to be.
12. Close up the date and repeat with the remaining dates.
13. Dip any exposed cheese from the stuffed dates into the reserved chopped pecans to cover it up.
14. Set the dates on a serving plate; serve immediately or chill in the fridge until you are ready to serve.

Mediterranean Trail Mix

Prep time: 5 minutes|Cook time:30 minutes|Serves 6

- 1 cup roughly chopped unsalted walnuts
- ½ cup roughly chopped salted almonds
- ½ cup shelled salted pistachios
- ½ cup roughly chopped apricots
- ½ cup roughly chopped dates
- ⅓ cup dried figs, rasherd in half

1. In a large zip-top bag, combine the walnuts, almonds, pistachios, apricots, dates, and figs and mix well.

Savory Mediterranean Popcorn

Prep time: 5 minutes|Cook time:2 minutes|Serves 4 to 6

- 3 tablespoons extra-virgin olive oil
- ¼ teaspoon garlic powder
- ¼ teaspoon freshly ground black pepper
- ¼ teaspoon sea salt
- ⅛ teaspoon dried thyme
- ⅛ teaspoon dried oregano
- 12 cups plain popped popcorn

1. In a large sauté pan or frying pan, heat the oil over medium heat, until shimmering, and then add the garlic powder, pepper, salt, thyme, and oregano until fragrant.
2. In a large bowl, drizzle the oil over the popcorn, toss, and serve.

Olive Tapenade with Anchovies

Prep time: 5 minutes | Cook time: 10 minutes, plus 1 hour | Serves 2

- 2 cups pitted Kalamata olives or other black olives
- 2 anchovy fillets, chopped
- 2 teaspoons chopped capers
- 1 garlic clove, finely minced
- 1 cooked egg yolk
- 1 teaspoon Dijon mustard
- ¼ cup extra-virgin olive oil
- Seedy Water biscuits, Versatile Sandwich Round, or vegetables, for serving (optional)

1. Rinse the olives in cold water and drain well.
2. In a food processor, blender, or a large jar (if using an immersion blender) place the drained olives, anchovies, capers, garlic, egg yolk, and Dijon.
3. Process until it forms a thick paste.
4. With the food processor running, slowly stream in the olive oil.
5. Transfer to a small bowl, cover, and refrigerate at least 1 hour to let the flavors develop.
6. Serve with Seedy Water biscuits, atop a Versatile Sandwich Round, or with your favorite crunchy vegetables.

Greek Deviled Eggs

Prep time: 15 minutes, plus 30 minutes | Cook time: 15 minutes | Serves 4

- 4 large hardboiled eggs
- 2 tablespoons Roasted Garlic Aioli or whole-milk Greek yogurt
- ½ cup finely crumbled feta cheese
- 8 pitted Kalamata olives, finely chopped
- 2 tablespoons chopped sun-dried tomatoes
- 1 tablespoon minced red onion
- ½ teaspoon dried dill
- ¼ teaspoon freshly ground black pepper

1. Rasher the hardboiled eggs in half lengthwise, remove the yolks, and place the yolks in a medium bowl.
2. Reserve the egg white halves and set aside.
3. Smash the yolks well with a fork.
4. Add the aioli, feta, olives, sun-dried tomatoes, onion, dill, and pepper and stir to combine until smooth and creamy.
5. Spoon the filling into each egg white half and chill for 30 minutes, or up to 24 hours, covered.

Homemade Sea Salt Pita Chips

Prep time: 2 minutes|Cook time:8 minutes|Serves 8

- 2 whole wheat pitas
- 1 tablespoon olive oil
- ½ teaspoon flaked salt

1. Preheat the air fryer to 180 .
2. Cut each pita into 8 wedges.
3. In a medium bowl, toss the pita wedges, olive oil, and salt until the wedges are coated and the olive oil and salt are evenly distributed.
4. Place the pita wedges into the air fryer basket in an even layer and fry for 6 to 8 minutes. (The cooking time will vary depending upon how thick the pita is and how browned you prefer a chip.)
5. Season with additional salt, if desired.
6. Serve alone or with a favorite dip.

Greek Potato Skins with Olives and Feta

Prep time: 5 minutes|Cook time:45 minutes|Serves 4

- 2 russet potatoes
- 3 tablespoons olive oil, divided, plus more for drizzling (optional)
- 1 teaspoon flaked salt , divided
- ¼ teaspoon black pepper
- 2 tablespoons fresh coriander, fresh, chopped, plus more for serving
- ¼ cup Kalamata olives, diced
- ¼ cup crumbled feta
- Chopped fresh parsley, for garnish (optional)

1. Preheat the air fryer to 190 .
2. Using a fork, poke 2 to 3 holes in the potatoes, then coat each with about ½ tablespoon olive oil and ½ teaspoon salt.
3. Place the potatoes into the air fryer basket and bake for 30 minutes.
4. Remove the potatoes from the air fryer, and rasher in half.
5. Using a spoon, scoop out the flesh of the potatoes, leaving a ½-inch layer of potato inside the skins, and set the skins aside.
6. In a medium bowl, combine the scooped potato middles with the remaining 2 tablespoons of olive oil, ½ teaspoon of salt, black pepper, and coriander, fresh.
7. Mix until well combined.
8. Divide the potato filling into the now-empty potato skins, spreading it evenly over them.
9. Top each potato with a tablespoon each of the olives and feta.
10. Place the loaded potato skins back into the air fryer and bake for 15 minutes.
11. Serve with additional chopped coriander, fresh or parsley and a drizzle of olive oil, if desired.

Arabil–Style Spiced Roasted Chickpeas

Prep time: 15 minutes | Cook time: 35 minutes | Serves 2

- For the seasoning mix
- ¾ teaspoon cumin
- ½ teaspoon coriander
- ½ teaspoon salt
- ¼ teaspoon freshly ground black pepper
- ¼ teaspoon paprika
- ¼ teaspoon cardamom
- ¼ teaspoon cinnamon
- ¼ teaspoon allspice
- For the chickpeas
- 1 (15-ounce) can chickpeas, drained and rinsed
- 1 tablespoon olive oil
- ¼ teaspoon salt

TO MAKE THE SEASONING MIX

1. In a small bowl, combine the cumin, coriander, salt, freshly ground black pepper, paprika, cardamom, cinnamon, and allspice.
2. Stir well to combine and set aside.

TO MAKE THE CHICKPEAS

1. Preheat the oven to 200 and set the rack to the middle position.
2. Line a baking tray with greaseproof paper.
3. Pat the rinsed chickpeas with paper towels or roll them in a clean kitchen towel to dry off any water.
4. Place the chickpeas in a bowl and season them with the olive oil and salt.
5. Add the chickpeas to the lined baking tray (reserve the bowl) and roast them for about 25 to 35 minutes, turning them over once or twice while cooking.
6. Most should be light brown.
7. Taste one or two to make sure they are slightly crisp.
8. Place the roasted chickpeas back into the bowl and sprinkle them with the seasoning mix.
9. Toss lightly to combine.
10. Taste, and add additional salt if needed.
11. Serve warm.

Apple Chips With Chocolate Tahini

Prep time: 10 minutes | Cook time: 30 minutes | Serves 2

- 2 tablespoons tahini
- 1 tablespoon maple syrup
- 1 tablespoon unsweetened cocoa powder
- 1 to 2 tablespoons warm water (or more if needed)
- 2 medium apples
- 1 tablespoon roasted, salted sunflower seeds

1. In a small bowl, mix together the tahini, maple syrup, and cocoa powder.
2. Add warm water, a little at a time, until thin enough to drizzle.
3. Do not microwave it to thin it—it won't work.
4. Rasher the apples crosswise into round rashers, and then cut each piece in half to make a chip.
5. Lay the apple chips out on a plate and drizzle them with the chocolate tahini sauce.
6. Sprinkle sunflower seeds over the apple chips.

Strawberry Caprese Skewers

Prep time: 15 minutes | Cook time: 30 minutes | Serves 2

- ½ cup balsamic vinegar
- 16 whole, hulled strawberries
- 12 small basil leaves or 6 large leaves, halved
- 12 pieces of small mozzarella balls (ciliegine)

1. To make the balsamic glaze, pour the balsamic vinegar into a small saucepan and bring it to a boil.
2. Reduce the heat to medium-low and simmer for 10 minutes, or until it's reduced by half and is thick enough to coat the back of a spoon.
3. On each of 4 wooden skewers, place a strawberry, a folded basil leaf, and a mozzarella ball, repeating twice and adding a strawberry on the end. (Each skewer should have 4 strawberries, 3 basil leaves, and 3 mozzarella balls.)
4. Drizzle 1 to 2 teaspoons of balsamic glaze over the skewers.

Rocket Salad with Figs, Prosciutto, Walnuts, and Parmesan

Prep time: 5 minutes | Cook time: 10 minutes | Serves 6

- ¼ cup extra-virgin olive oil
- 2 ounces thinly rasherd prosciutto, cut into ¼-inch-wide ribbons
- 3 tablespoons balsamic vinegar
- 1 tablespoon raspberry jam
- 1 small shallot, minced
- Salt and pepper
- ½ cup dried figs, stemmed and chopped
- 8 ounces (8 cups) baby rocket
- ½ cup walnuts, toasted and chopped
- 2 ounces Parmesan cheese, shaved

1. Heat 1 tablespoon oil in 10-inch nonstick frying pan over medium heat.
2. Add prosciutto and cook, stirring often, until crisp, about 7 minutes.
3. Using slotted spoon, transfer prosciutto to paper towel–lined plate; set aside.
4. Whisk vinegar, jam, shallot, ¼ teaspoon salt, and ⅛ teaspoon pepper together in large bowl.
5. Stir in figs, cover, and microwave until steaming, about 1 minute.
6. Whisking constantly, slowly drizzle in remaining 3 tablespoons oil.
7. Let sit until figs are softened and vinaigrette has cooled to room temperature, about 15 minutes.
8. Just before serving, whisk vinaigrette to re-emulsify.
9. Add rocket and gently toss to coat.
10. Season with salt and pepper to taste.
11. Serve, topping individual portions with prosciutto, walnuts, and Parmesan.

Rocket Salad with Pear, Almonds, Goat Cheese, and Apricots

Prep time: 5 minutes | Cook time: 10 minutes | Serves 6

- 3 tablespoons white wine vinegar
- 1 tablespoon apricot jam
- 1 small shallot, minced
- Salt and pepper
- ½ cup dried apricots, chopped
- 3 tablespoons extra-virgin olive oil
- ¼ small red onion, rasherd thin
- 8 ounces (8 cups) baby rocket
- 1 ripe but firm pear, halved, cored, and rasherd ¼ inch thick
- ⅓ cup rasherd almonds, toasted
- 3 ounces goat cheese, crumbled (¾ cup)

1. Whisk vinegar, jam, shallot, ¼ teaspoon salt, and ⅛ teaspoon pepper together in large bowl.
2. Add apricots, cover, and microwave until steaming, about 1 minute.
3. Whisking constantly, slowly drizzle in oil.
4. Stir in onion and let sit until figs are softened and vinaigrette has cooled to room temperature, about 15 minutes.
5. Just before serving, whisk vinaigrette to re-emulsify.
6. Add rocket and pear and gently toss to coat.
7. Season with salt and pepper to taste.
8. Serve, topping individual portions with almonds and goat cheese.

Chapter 6
Chicken and Poultry

Italian Chicken Thighs with Mushrooms
Prep time: 5 minutes|Cook time:25 minutes|Serves 2

- 2 chicken thighs, boneless and skinless
- 6 oz button mushrooms
- 3 tbsp olive oil
- 1 tsp fresh rosemary, finely chopped
- 2 garlic cloves, crushed
- ½ tsp salt
- 1 tbsp butter
- 1 tbsp Italian Seasoning mix

1. Heat a tablespoon of olive oil on Sauté.
2. Add chicken thighs and sear for 5 minutes. Set aside.
3. Pour in the remaining oil, and add mushrooms, rosemary, and Italian seasoning mix.
4. Stir-fry for 5 minutes.
5. Add in butter, chicken, and 2 cups of water.
6. Seal the lid and cook on Pressure Cook mode for 13 minutes on High.
7. Do a quick release.
8. Remove the chicken and mushrooms from the cooker and serve with onions.

Chicken in Orange Gravy
Prep time: 5 minutes|Cook time:20 minutes|Serves 4

- 1 tbsp olive oil
- 4 boneless, skinless chicken thighs,
- ¼ cup orange juice
- 2 tbsp tomato sauce
- 2 tbsp Worcestershire sauce
- 1 garlic clove, minced
- 1 tsp cornflour
- 2 tsp water
- A handful of fresh coriander, fresh, chopped

1. Warm oil on Sauté. In batches, sear chicken in oil for 3 minutes until golden brown; set aside on a plate.
2. Mix orange juice, Worcestershire sauce, garlic, and tomato sauce; add to the pot to deglaze, scrape the bottom to get rid of any browned bits of food.
3. Place the chicken into the sauce and stir well to coat.
4. Seal the lid cook for 5 minutes on High Pressure.
5. Release the Pressure quickly.
6. In a small bowl, mix water and cornflour until well dissolved.
7. Press Cancel and set to Sauté mode.
8. Stir the cornflour slurry into the sauce; cook for 2 minutes until the sauce is well thickened.
9. Serve in bowls with coriander, fresh.

Turkey with Rigatoni
Prep time: 5 minutes|Cook time:35 minutes|Serves 4

- 2 tbsp Rapeseed oil
- 1 pound ground turkey
- 1 egg
- ¼ cup bread crumbs
- 2 cloves garlic, minced
- 1 tsp dried oregano
- Salt and ground black pepper to taste
- 3 cups tomato sauce
- ounces rigatoni
- 2 tbsp grated Grana Padano cheese

1. In a bowl, combine turkey, crumbs, cumin, garlic, and egg.
2. Season with oregano, salt, red pepper flakes, and pepper.
3. Form the mixture into meatballs with well-oiled hands.
4. Warm the oil on Sauté.
5. Cook the meatballs for 3 to 4 minutes, until browned on all sides.
6. Remove to a plate.
7. Add rigatoni to the cooker and cover with tomato sauce.
8. Pour enough water to cover the pasta. Stir well. Throw in the meatballs.
9. Seal the lid and cook for 10 minutes on High Pressure.
10. Release the Pressure quickly.
11. Serve topped with Grana Padano cheese.

Greek Turkey Meatballs
Prep time: 5 minutes|Cook time:25 minutes|Serves 6

- 1 onion, minced
- ½ cup plain bread crumbs
- ⅓ cup feta cheese, crumbled
- 2 tsp salt
- ½ tsp dried oregano
- ¼ tsp ground black pepper
- 1 pound ground turkey
- 1 egg, lightly beaten
- 1 tbsp olive oil
- 1 carrot, minced
- ½ celery stalk, minced
- 3 cups tomato puree
- 2 cups water

1. In a mixing bowl, combine half the onion, oregano, turkey, salt, crumbs, pepper, and egg, and stir until everything is well incorporated.
2. Heat oil on Sauté mode, and cook celery, remaining onion, and carrot for 5 minutes, until soft.
3. Pour in water, and tomato puree. Adjust the seasonings.
4. Roll the mixture into meatballs, and drop into the sauce. Seal the lid.
5. Press Meat/Stew and cook on High Pressure for 5 minutes.
6. Allow the cooker to cool and release the pressure naturally for 20 minutes.
7. Serve topped with feta cheese.

Chicken with Salsa Verde
Prep time: 5 minutes|Cook time:45 minutes|Serves 4

- Salsa Verde:
- 1 jalapeño pepper, deveined and chopped
- ½ cup capers
- ¼ cup parsley
- 1 Lime, juiced
- 1 tsp salt
- ¼ cup extra virgin olive oil
- Chicken:
- 4 boneless skinless chicken breasts
- 2 cups water
- 1 cup rice, rinsed

1. In a blender, mix olive oil, salt, lime juice, jalapeño pepper, capers, and parsley and blend until smooth.
2. Arrange chicken breasts at the bottom of the cooker.
3. Over the chicken, add salsa verde mixture.
4. In a bowl that can fit in the cooker, mix rice and water.
5. Set a steamer rack onto chicken and sauce.
6. Set the bowl onto the rack. Seal the lid and cook on High Pressure for 20 minutes. Release the Pressure quickly.
7. Remove the rice bowl and rack.
8. Using two forks, shred chicken into the sauce; stir to coat.
9. Divide the rice, between plates.
10. Top with chicken and salsa verde before serving.

Chicken with Mixed Vegetables
Prep time: 20 minutes|Cook time:20 minutes|Serves 2

- 1/2 onion diced
- Chicken breast: 4 cups, cubed pieces
- Half Courgette chopped
- Italian seasoning: 1 tablespoon
- Bell pepper chopped: 1/2 cup
- Clove of garlic pressed
- Broccoli florets: 1/2 cup
- Olive oil: 2 tablespoons
- Half teaspoon of Chili con carne powder, garlic powder, pepper, salt

1. Preheat the Air Fryer to 200 and dice the vegetables.
2. In a bowl, add the seasoning, oil, vegetables, and chicken and toss well.
3. Place chicken and vegetables in the Air Fryer, and cook for ten minutes, tossing halfway through, cook in batches.
4. Make sure the veggies are charred, and the chicken is cooked through.

Greek Chicken Meatballs
Prep time: 10 minutes|Cook time:15 minutes|Serves 2

- 1 lb. ground chicken
- 1 tsp. Greek seasoning
- 1/2 oz. finely ground scratchings
- 1/3 cup feta, crumbled
- 1/3 cup frozen spinach, drained and thawed
- Tzatziki

1. Place all ingredients in a large bowl, and combine with your hands.
2. Take equal-sized portions of this mixture and roll each into a 2-inch ball.
3. Place the balls in your Air Fryer.
4. Cook the meatballs at 175 for 12 minutes in several batches.
5. Once they are golden, ensure they have reached an ideal temperature of 85 and remove it from the Air Fryer.
6. Keep each batch warm and serve with Tzatziki.

Roasted Red Pepper Chicken with Lemony Garlic Hummus
Prep time: 10 minutes|Cook time:10 minutes|Serves 6

- 1¼ pounds boneless, skinless chicken thighs, cut into 1-inch pieces
- ½ sweet or red onion, cut into 1-inch chunks (about 1 cup)
- 2 tablespoons extra-virgin olive oil
- ½ teaspoon dried thyme
- ¼ teaspoon freshly ground black pepper
- ¼ teaspoon kosher or sea salt
- 1 (12-ounce) jar roasted red peppers, drained and chopped
- Lemony Garlic Hummus, or a 10-ounce container prepared hummus
- ½ medium lemon
- 3 (6-inch) whole-wheat pita breads, cut into eighths

1. Line a large, rimmed baking tray with Aluminium foil. Set aside.
2. Set one oven rack about 4 inches below the broiler element.
3. Preheat the broiler to high.
4. In a large bowl, mix together the chicken, onion, oil, thyme, pepper, and salt.
5. Spread the mixture onto the prepared baking tray.
6. Place the chicken under the broiler and broil for 5 minutes.
7. Remove the pan, stir in the red peppers, and return to the broiler. Broil for another 5 minutes, or until the chicken and onion just start to char on the tips. Remove from the oven.
8. Spread the hummus onto a large serving platter, and spoon the chicken mixture on top.
9. Squeeze the juice from half a lemon over the top, and serve with the pita pieces.

Tahini Chicken Rice Bowls

Prep time: 10 minutes|Cook time:15 minutes|Serves 4

- 1 cup uncooked instant brown rice
- ¼ cup tahini or ground nut butter (tahini for nut-free)
- ¼ cup 2% plain Greek yogurt
- 2 tablespoons chopped spring onions, green and white parts (2 spring onions)
- 1 tablespoon freshly squeezed lemon juice (from ½ medium lemon)
- 1 tablespoon water
- 1 teaspoon ground cumin
- ¾ teaspoon ground cinnamon
- ¼ teaspoon kosher or sea salt
- 2 cups chopped cooked chicken breast (about 1 pound)
- ½ cup chopped dried apricots
- 2 cups peeled and chopped seedless cucumber (1 large cucumber)
- 4 teaspoons sesame seeds
- Fresh mint leaves, for serving (optional)

1. Cook the brown rice according to the package instructions.
2. While the rice is cooking, in a medium bowl, mix together the tahini, yogurt, spring onions, lemon juice, water, cumin, cinnamon, and salt.
3. Transfer half the tahini mixture to another medium bowl.
4. Mix the chicken into the first bowl.
5. When the rice is done, mix it into the second bowl of tahini (the one without the chicken).
6. To assemble, divide the chicken among four bowls.
7. Spoon the rice mixture next to the chicken in each bowl.
8. Next to the chicken, place the dried apricots, and in the remaining empty section, add the cucumbers.
9. Sprinkle with sesame seeds, and top with mint, if desired, and serve.

Garlic-Lemon Chicken and Potatoes

Prep time: 10 minutes|Cook time:45 minutes|Serves 4 to 6

- 1 cup garlic, minced
- 1½ cups lemon juice
- 1 cup plus 2 tablespoons extra-virgin olive oil, divided
- 1½ teaspoons salt, divided
- 1 teaspoon freshly ground black pepper
- 1 whole chicken, cut into 8 pieces
- 1 pound fingerling or red potatoes

1. Preheat the oven to 200 .
2. In a large bowl, whisk together the garlic, lemon juice, 1 cup of olive oil, 1 teaspoon of salt, and pepper.
3. Put the chicken in a large baking dish and pour half of the lemon sauce over the chicken. Cover the baking dish with foil, and cook for 20 minutes.
4. Cut the potatoes in half, and toss to coat with 2 tablespoons olive oil and 1 teaspoon of salt.
5. Put them on a baking tray and bake for 20 minutes in the same oven as the chicken.
6. Take both the chicken and potatoes out of the oven.
7. Using a spatula, transfer the potatoes to the baking dish with the chicken.
8. Pour the remaining sauce over the potatoes and chicken. Bake for another 25 minutes.
9. Transfer the chicken and potatoes to a serving dish and spoon the garlic-lemon sauce from the pan on top.

Whole-Roasted Spanish Chicken

Prep time: 1 hours|Cook time:45 minutes|Serves 4

- 4 tablespoons (½ stick) unsalted butter, softened
- 2 tablespoons lemon zest
- 2 tablespoons smoked paprika
- 2 tablespoons garlic, minced
- 1½ teaspoons salt
- 1 teaspoon freshly ground black pepper
- 1 5-pound whole chicken, skin on

1. In a small bowl, combine the butter with the lemon zest, paprika, garlic, salt, and pepper.
2. Pat the chicken dry using a paper towel.
3. Using your hands, rub the seasoned butter all over the chicken.
4. Refrigerate the chicken for 30 minutes.
5. Preheat the oven to 225 . Take the chicken out of the fridge and let it sit out for 20 minutes.
6. Put the chicken in a baking dish in the oven and let it cook for 20 minutes. Turn the temperature down to 175 and let the chicken cook for another 35 minutes.
7. Take the chicken out of the oven and let it stand for 10 minutes before serving.

Lemon-Pepper Chicken Thighs

Prep time: 5 minutes|Cook time:22 minutes|Serves 4

- 4 bone-in chicken thighs, skin and fat removed
- 2 tablespoons olive oil
- 1 teaspoon garlic powder
- 1 teaspoon salt
- Black pepper
- 1 lemon, rasherd

1. Preheat the air fryer to 190 .
2. Coat the chicken thighs in the olive oil, garlic powder, and salt.
3. Tear off four pieces of Aluminium foil, with each sheet being large enough to envelop one chicken thigh.
4. Place one chicken thigh onto each piece of foil, season it with black pepper, and then top it with rashers of lemon.
5. Bake for 20 to 22 minutes, or until the internal temperature of the chicken has reached 180 .
6. Remove the foil packets from the air fryer. Carefully open each packet to avoid a steam burn.

Sweet and Savory Stuffed Chicken

Prep time: 10 minutes | Cook time: 20 minutes | Serves 4

- ⅓ cup cooked brown rice
- 1 teaspoon mixed Spice Rub
- 4 (6-ounce) boneless skinless chicken breasts
- 1 tablespoon harissa
- 3 tablespoons extra-virgin olive oil, divided
- Salt
- Freshly ground black pepper
- 4 small dried apricots, halved
- ⅓ cup crumbled feta
- 1 tablespoon chopped fresh parsley

1. Preheat the oven to 185.
2. In a medium bowl, mix the rice and shawarma seasoning and set aside.
3. Butterfly the chicken breasts by slicing them almost in half, starting at the thickest part and folding them open like a book.
4. In a small bowl, mix the harissa with 1 tablespoon of olive oil.
5. Brush the chicken with the harissa oil and season with salt and pepper.
6. The harissa adds a nice heat, so feel free to add a thicker coating for more spice.
7. Onto one side of each chicken breast, spoon 1 to 2 tablespoons of rice, then layer 2 apricot halves in each breast.
8. Divide the feta between the chicken breasts and fold the other side over the filling to close.
9. In an oven-safe sauté pan or frying pan, heat the remaining 2 tablespoons of olive oil and sear the breast for 2 minutes on each side, then place the pan into the oven for 15 minutes, or until fully cooked and juices run clear.
10. Serve, garnished with parsley.

Spicy Turkey Meatballs

Prep time: 5 minutes | Cook time: 12 minutes | Serves 4

- 1 pound ground turkey
- 1 egg
- ¼ teaspoon red pepper flakes
- ¼ cup whole wheat bread crumbs
- 1 teaspoon salt
- ½ teaspoon garlic powder
- ½ teaspoon onion powder
- ½ teaspoon black pepper

1. Preheat the air fryer to 180.
2. In a large bowl, combine all of the ingredients and mix well.
3. Divide the meatball mixture into 12 portions.
4. Roll each portion into a ball and place into the bottom of the air fryer basket, making sure that they don't touch each other.
5. Cook for 10 to 12 minutes, or until the meatballs are cooked through and browned.

Spinach and Feta Stuffed Chicken

Prep time: 10 minutes | Cook time: 25 minutes | Serves 2

- 4 tablespoons extra-virgin olive oil, divided
- ½ cup chopped shallots
- 1 lemon, zested and juiced
- 1 garlic clove, minced
- ⅓ cup chopped baby spinach
- ½ cup crumbled feta cheese
- 4 finely chopped pitted kalamata olives
- Salt
- Freshly ground black pepper
- 2 boneless, skinless chicken breasts
- 2 teaspoons whole-wheat flour

1. Preheat the oven to 170.
2. In an oven-safe, nonstick sauté pan or frying pan, heat 2 tablespoons of olive oil over medium heat until it shimmers.
3. Add the shallots and cook for 3 to 5 minutes, until translucent.
4. Add the lemon zest and juice and garlic and heat for about 1 minute, until fragrant.
5. Add the spinach and stir for 3 to 5 minutes, until heated through and most of the water is cooked out of the spinach.
6. Transfer the spinach-shallot mixture to a bowl.
7. Wipe the frying pan clean and set aside.
8. Stir the feta cheese and olives into the spinach mixture. Season with salt and pepper.
9. Butterfly the chicken breasts by slicing them almost in half, starting at the thickest part, and folding them open like a book.
10. Make sure not to cut all the way through. Season with salt and pepper.
11. Onto one side of each chicken breast, place half of the shallot and spinach mixture and fold the other side over the filling to close.
12. Use toothpicks to hold the sides together.
13. Dust the chicken lightly with flour, salt, and pepper.
14. Return the frying pan to high heat and sear the stuffed chicken for 2 minutes on each side.
15. If the pan looks dry, add the remaining 2 tablespoons of olive oil to the pan while it's cooking.
16. Once all sides are seared, put the pan in the oven.
17. Bake for 15 to 20 minutes, or until the breasts are cooked through and juices run clear

One-Pan Harissa Chicken and Brussels Sprouts with Yogurt Sauce

Prep time: 10 minutes | Cook time: 1 hours | Serves 4

- 8 tablespoons extra-virgin olive oil, divided
- 2 tablespoons Harissa Oil or a store-bought harissa
- 1½ teaspoons salt, divided
- ½ teaspoon ground cumin
- 4 skin-on, bone-in chicken thighs (or a combination of thighs and drumsticks)
- 1 pound Brussels sprouts, ends trimmed and halved
- ½ cup plain whole-milk Greek yogurt
- 1 garlic clove, finely minced
- Zest and juice of 1 lemon
- ½ cup chopped mint leaves, for serving
- ½ cup chopped coriander, fresh leaves, for serving

1. Preheat the oven to 215.
2. Line a rimmed baking tray with Aluminium foil. (Alternatively, you can use a 9-by-13-inch glass baking dish and skip the foil.)
3. In a small bowl, whisk together 6 tablespoons olive oil, the harissa oil, 1 teaspoon salt, and cumin.
4. Place the chicken in a large bowl and drizzle half of the harissa mixture over top. Toss to combine well.
5. Place the chicken in a single layer on the prepared baking tray and roast for 20 minutes.
6. While the chicken roasts, place the Brussels sprouts in a large bowl and drizzle with the remaining harissa mixture.
7. Toss to combine well. After the chicken has roasted for 20 minutes, remove from the oven and add the Brussels sprouts to the baking tray in a single layer around the chicken.
8. Return to the oven and continue to roast until the chicken is cooked through and the Brussels sprouts are golden and crispy, another 20 to 25 minutes.
9. In a small bowl, combine the yogurt, remaining 2 tablespoons olive oil, garlic, lemon zest and juice, and remaining ½ teaspoon salt and whisk to combine.
10. When the chicken and Brussels sprouts have finished cooking, remove from the oven and cool for 10 minutes.
11. Drizzle with yogurt sauce and sprinkle with mint and coriander, fresh.
12. Toss to combine and serve warm.

Chicken Piccata with Mushrooms

Prep time: 25 minutes | Cook time: 25 minutes | Serves 4

- 1 pound thinly rasherd chicken breasts
- 1½ teaspoons salt, divided
- ½ teaspoon freshly ground black pepper
- ¼ cup ground flaxseed
- 2 tablespoons almond flour
- 8 tablespoons extra-virgin olive oil, divided
- 4 tablespoons butter, divided
- 2 cups rasherd mushrooms
- ½ cup dry white wine or chicken stock
- ¼ cup freshly squeezed lemon juice
- ¼ cup roughly chopped capers
- Courgette Noodles, for serving
- ¼ cup chopped fresh flat-leaf Italian parsley, for garnish

1. Season the chicken with 1 teaspoon salt and the pepper.
2. On a plate, combine the ground flaxseed and almond flour and dredge each chicken breast in the mixture. Set aside.
3. In a large frying pan, heat 4 tablespoons olive oil and 1 tablespoon butter over medium-high heat.
4. Working in batches if necessary, brown the chicken, 3 to 4 minutes per side. Remove from the frying pan and keep warm.
5. Add the remaining 4 tablespoons olive oil and 1 tablespoon butter to the frying pan along with mushrooms and sauté over medium heat until just tender, 6 to 8 minutes.
6. Serve chicken and mushrooms warm over Courgette Noodles, spooning the mushroom sauce over top and garnishing with chopped parsley.

Bruschetta Chicken Burgers

Prep time: 15 minutes | Cook time: 15 minutes | Serves 2

- 1 tablespoon olive oil
- 3 tablespoons finely minced onion
- 2 garlic cloves, minced
- 1 teaspoon dried basil
- ¼ teaspoon salt
- 3 tablespoons minced sun-dried tomatoes packed in olive oil
- 8 ounces ground chicken breast
- 3 pieces small mozzarella balls (ciliegine), minced

1. Heat the grill to high heat (about 200) and oil the grill grates.
2. Alternatively, you can cook these in a nonstick frying pan.
3. Heat the olive oil in a small frying pan over medium-high heat.
4. Add the onion and garlic and sauté for 5 minutes, until softened.
5. Stir in the basil. Remove from the heat and place in a medium bowl.
6. Add the salt, sun-dried tomatoes, and ground chicken and stir to combine. Mix in the mozzarella balls.
7. Divide the chicken mixture in half and form into two burgers, each about ¾-inch thick.
8. Place the burgers on the grill and cook for five minutes, or until golden on the bottom.
9. Flip the burgers over and grill for another five minutes, or until they reach an internal temperature of 85.
10. If cooking the burgers in a frying pan on the stovetop, heat a nonstick frying pan over medium-high heat and add the burgers.
11. Cook them for 5 to 6 minutes on the first side, or until golden brown on the bottom.
12. Flip the burgers and cook for an additional 5 minutes, or until they reach an internal temperature of 85.

Chapter 7
Beef, Lamb and Pork

Jalapeño Pork

Prep time: 5 minutes | Cook time: 55 minutes | Serves 4

- 1 lb pork shoulder
- 2 tbsp olive oil
- 3 Jalapeño peppers, seeded and finely chopped
- 1 tsp ground cumin
- 3 cups water
- 1 large onion, roughly chopped
- 2 garlic cloves, crushed
- 3 cups beef broth

1. Heat oil on Sauté and cook the jalapeno peppers for 3 minutes.
2. Add in all the spices, garlic and onion and stir-fry for another 2 minutes, until soft.
3. Add in the pork shoulder, beef broth and the pureed mixture.
4. Seal the lid, and cook on Meat/Stew for 30 minutes on High.
5. Release the pressure quickly and serve hot.

Dinner Pork Roast

Prep time: 5 minutes | Cook time: 40 minutes | Serves 6

- 3 pounds Rump steak Pork Roast
- 1 tbsp Honey
- 1 tsp Chili con carne Powder
- 1 tbsp Rosemary
- 1 tbsp Olive Oil
- 1¼ cups Water
- 2 tbsp Lemon Juice

1. Combine the spices, in a bowl, and rub them onto the pork.
2. Heat oil on SAUTÉ mode and sear the pork on all sides.
3. Stir in the remaining ingredients and seal the lid.
4. Cook for 30 minutes, on MEAT/STEW at High.
5. Do a natural pressure release, for 15 minutes.

Basil-Flavored Pork Stew

Prep time: 5 minutes | Cook time: 40 minutes | Serves 4

- 16 oz pork fillet, cut into bite-sized pieces
- 1 onion, peeled, chopped
- 2 tbsp vegetable oil
- 4 tomatoes, peeled, diced
- ½ tbsp red wine
- ½ tbsp beef broth
- A handful of fresh basil
- 1 tsp salt
- ¼ tsp pepper

1. Heat oil and stir-fry the onions, until translucent.
2. Add the meat, salt, pepper, wine, and basil. Cook for 10 minutes.
3. Pour in broth, seal the lid and cook on High Pressure for 25 minutes. Do a quick release.
4. Do a quick release. Season with salt, pepper, and red pepper flakes.
5. Add butter and cook until the liquid evaporates – for 10 minutes, on Sauté mode.

Beef & Vegetable Stew

Prep time: 5 minutes | Cook time: 30 minutes | Serves 6

- 2 lb beef meat for stew
- ¾ cup red wine
- 1 tbsp ghee
- 6 oz tomato paste
- 6 oz baby carrots, chopped
- 2 sweet potatoes, cut into chunks
- 1 onion, finely chopped
- ½ tsp salt
- 4 cups beef broth
- ½ cup green peas
- 1 tsp dried thyme
- 3 garlic cloves, crushed

1. Heat the ghee on Sauté. Add beef and brown for 5-6 minutes.
2. Add onions and garlic, and keep stirring for 3 more minutes.
3. Add the remaining ingredients and seal the lid.
4. Cook on Meat/Stew for 20 minutes on High pressure.
5. Do a quick release and serve immediately.

Meatballs with Marinara Sauce

Prep time: 5 minutes | Cook time: 30 minutes | Serves 6

- 1½ pounds minced beef
- ⅓ cup warm water
- ¾ cup grated Parmigiano-Reggiano cheese
- ½ cup bread crumbs
- 1 egg
- 2 tbsp fresh parsley
- ¼ tsp garlic powder
- ¼ tsp dried oregano
- Salt and ground black pepper to taste
- ½ cup capers
- 1 tsp olive oil
- 3 cups marinara sauce

1. In a bowl, mix minced beef, garlic powder, pepper, oregano, crumbs, egg, and salt; shape into meatballs.
2. Warm oil on Sauté mode. Add meatballs to the oil and brown for 2-3 minutes and all sides.
3. Pour water and marinara sauce over the meatballs.
4. Seal the lid and cook on High Pressure for 10 minutes.
5. Release the Pressure quickly.
6. Serve in large bowls topped with capers and Parmigiano-Reggiano cheese.

Italian-Style Pot Roast

Prep time: 5 minutes | Cook time: 1 hours 30 minutes | Serves 5

- 2 ½ pounds beef brisket, trimmed
- Salt and freshly ground black pepper
- 2 tbsp olive oil
- 1 onion, chopped
- 3 garlic cloves, minced
- 1 cup beef broth
- ¾ cup dry red wine
- 2 fresh thyme sprigs
- 2 fresh rosemary sprigs
- 4 ounces pancetta, chopped
- 6 carrots, chopped
- 1 bay leaf
- A handful of parsley, chopped

1. Warm oil on Sauté. Fry the pancetta for 4-5 minutes until crispy. Set aside.
2. Season the beef with pepper and salt, and brown for 5 to 7 minutes per each.
3. Remove and set aside on a plate.
4. In the same oil, fry garlic and onion for 3 minutes until soften.
5. Pour in red wine and beef broth to deglaze the bottom, scrape the bottom of the pot to get rid of any browned bits of food.
6. Return the beef and pancetta to the pot and add rosemary sprigs and thyme.
7. Seal the lid and cook for 50 minutes on High Pressure. Release the Pressure quickly.
8. Add carrots and bay leaf to the pot. Seal the lid and cook for an additional 4 minutes on High Pressure.
9. Release the Pressure quickly.
10. Get rid of the thyme, bay leaf and rosemary sprigs.
11. Place beef on a serving plate and sprinkle with parsley to serve.

Grilled Steak, Mushroom, and Onion Kebabs

Prep time: 10 minutes | Cook time: 10 minutes | Serves 4

- Nonstick cooking spray
- 4 garlic cloves, peeled
- 2 fresh rosemary sprigs (about 3 inches each)
- 2 tablespoons extra-virgin olive oil, divided
- 1 pound boneless top rump steak steak, about 1 inch thick
- 1 (8-ounce) package white button mushrooms
- 1 medium red onion, cut into 12 thin wedges
- ¼ teaspoon coarsely ground black pepper
- 2 tablespoons red wine vinegar
- ¼ teaspoon kosher or sea salt

1. Soak 12 (10-inch) wooden skewers in water.
2. Spray the cold grill with nonstick cooking spray, and heat the grill to medium-high.
3. Cut a piece of Aluminium foil into a 10-inch square.
4. Place the garlic and rosemary sprigs in the center, drizzle with 1 tablespoon of oil, and wrap tightly to form a foil packet.
5. Place it on the grill, and close the grill cover.
6. Cut the steak into 1-inch cubes. Thread the beef onto the wet skewers, alternating with whole mushrooms and onion wedges.
7. Spray the kebabs thoroughly with nonstick cooking spray, and sprinkle with pepper.
8. Cook the kebabs on the covered grill for 4 to 5 minutes.
9. Turn and grill 4 to 5 more minutes, covered, until a meat thermometer inserted in the meat registers 75 (medium rare) or 80 (medium).
10. Remove the foil packet from the grill, open, and, using tongs, place the garlic and rosemary sprigs in a small bowl.
11. Carefully strip the rosemary sprigs of their leaves into the bowl and pour in any accumulated juices and oil from the foil packet.
12. Add the remaining 1 tablespoon of oil and the vinegar and salt.
13. Mash the garlic with a fork, and mix all ingredients in the bowl together.
14. Pour over the finished steak kebabs and serve.

Smoky Herb Lamb Cutlets and Lemon-Rosemary Dressing

Prep time: 1 hours 35 minutes | Cook time: 10 minutes | Serves 6

- 4 large cloves garlic
- 1 cup lemon juice
- ⅓ cup fresh rosemary
- 1 cup extra-virgin olive oil
- 1½ teaspoons salt
- 1 teaspoon freshly ground black pepper
- 6 1-inch-thick lamb cutlets

1. In a food processor or blender, blend the garlic, lemon juice, rosemary, olive oil, salt, and black pepper for 15 seconds. Set aside.
2. Put the lamb cutlets in a large plastic zip-top bag or container.
3. Cover the lamb with two-thirds of the rosemary dressing, making sure that all of the lamb cutlets are coated with the dressing.
4. Let the lamb marinate in the fridge for 1 hour.
5. When you are almost ready to eat, take the lamb cutlets out of the fridge and let them sit on the counter-top for 20 minutes.
6. Preheat a grill, grill pan, or lightly oiled frying pan to high heat.
7. Cook the lamb cutlets for 3 minutes on each side.
8. To serve, drizzle the lamb with the remaining dressing.

Beef Kebabs with Tahini Sauce

Prep time: 15 minutes | Cook time: 10 minutes | Serves 4

- Nonstick cooking spray
- 2 tablespoons extra-virgin olive oil
- 1 tablespoon dried oregano
- 1¼ teaspoons garlic powder, divided
- 1 teaspoon ground cumin
- ½ teaspoon freshly ground black pepper
- ¼ teaspoon kosher or sea salt
- 1 pound beef skirt steak, top chuck steak, or lamb leg steak, center cut, about 1 inch thick
- 1 medium green bell pepper, halved and seeded
- 2 tablespoons tahini or ground nut butter (tahini for nut-free)
- 1 tablespoon hot water (if needed)
- ½ cup 2% plain Greek yogurt
- 1 tablespoon freshly squeezed lemon juice (about ½ small lemon)
- 1 cup thinly rasherd red onion (about ½ onion)
- 4 (6-inch) whole-wheat pita breads, warmed

1. Set an oven rack about 4 inches below the broiler element.
2. Preheat the oven broiler to high. Line a large, rimmed baking tray with foil.
3. Place a wire cooling rack on the foil, and spray the rack with nonstick cooking spray. Set aside.
4. In a small bowl, whisk together the oil, oregano, 1 teaspoon of garlic powder, cumin, pepper, and salt.
5. Rub the oil mixture on all sides of the steak, saving 1 teaspoon of the mixture.
6. Place the steak on the prepared rack.
7. Rub the remaining oil mixture on the bell pepper, and place on the rack, cut-side down.
8. Press the pepper with the heel of your hand to flatten.
9. Broil for 5 minutes. Turn the meat and the pepper pieces, and broil for 2 to 5 more minutes, until the pepper is charred and the internal temperature of the meat measures 70 on a meat thermometer.
10. Put the pepper and steak on a cutting board to rest for 5 minutes.
11. While the meat is broiling, in a small bowl, whisk the tahini until smooth (adding 1 tablespoon of hot water if your tahini is sticky).
12. Add the remaining ¼ teaspoon of garlic powder and the yogurt and lemon juice, and whisk thoroughly.
13. Rasher the steak crosswise into ¼-inch-thick strips.
14. Rasher the bell pepper into strips.
15. Divide the steak, bell pepper, and onion among the warm pita breads.
16. Drizzle with tahini sauce and serve.

Seasoned Beef Kebabs

Prep time: 15 minutes | Cook time: 10 minutes | Serves 6

- 2 pounds beef fillet
- 1½ teaspoons salt
- 1 teaspoon freshly ground black pepper
- ½ teaspoon ground allspice
- ½ teaspoon ground nutmeg
- ⅓ cup extra-virgin olive oil
- 1 large onion, cut into 8 quarters
- 1 large red bell pepper, cut into 1-inch cubes

1. Preheat a grill, grill pan, or lightly oiled frying pan to high heat.
2. Cut the beef into 1-inch cubes and put them in a large bowl.
3. In a small bowl, mix together the salt, black pepper, allspice, and nutmeg.
4. Pour the olive oil over the beef and toss to coat the beef. Then evenly sprinkle the seasoning over the beef and toss to coat all pieces.
5. Skewer the beef, alternating every 1 or 2 pieces with a piece of onion or bell pepper.
6. To cook, place the skewers on the grill or frying pan, and turn every 2 to 3 minutes until all sides have cooked to desired doneness, 6 minutes for medium-rare, 8 minutes for well done.
7. Serve warm.

Garlic Pork Fillet and Lemony Orzo

Prep time: 15 minutes | Cook time: 20 minutes | Serves 6

- 1 pound pork fillet
- ½ teaspoon mixed Spice Rub
- 1 tablespoon salt
- ½ teaspoon coarsely ground black pepper
- ½ teaspoon garlic powder
- 6 tablespoons extra-virgin olive oil
- 3 cups Lemony Orzo

1. Preheat the oven to 170 .
2. Rub the pork with shawarma seasoning, salt, pepper, and garlic powder and drizzle with the olive oil.
3. Put the pork on a baking tray and roast for 20 minutes, or until desired doneness.
4. Remove the pork from the oven and let rest for 10 minutes.
5. Assemble the pork on a plate with the orzo and enjoy.

Roasted Pork with Apple-Dijon Sauce

Prep time: 15 minutes | Cook time: 40 minutes | Serves 8

- 1½ tablespoons extra-virgin olive oil
- 1 (12-ounce) pork fillet
- ¼ teaspoon flaked salt
- ¼ teaspoon freshly ground black pepper
- ¼ cup apple jelly
- ¼ cup apple juice
- 2 to 3 tablespoons Dijon mustard
- ½ tablespoon cornflour
- ½ tablespoon cream

1. Preheat the oven to 105 .
2. In a large sauté pan or frying pan, heat the olive oil over medium heat.
3. Add the pork to the frying pan, using tongs to turn and sear the pork on all sides.
4. Once seared, sprinkle pork with salt and pepper, and set it on a small baking tray.
5. In the same frying pan, with the juices from the pork, mix the apple jelly, juice, and mustard into the pan juices.
6. Heat thoroughly over low heat, stirring consistently for 5 minutes. Spoon over the pork.
7. Put the pork in the oven and roast for 15 to 17 minutes, or 20 minutes per pound.
8. Every 10 to 15 minutes, baste the pork with the apple-mustard sauce.
9. Once the pork fillet is done, remove it from the oven and let it rest for 15 minutes. Then, cut it into 1-inch rashers.
10. In a small pot, blend the cornflour with cream. Heat over low heat. Add the pan juices into the pot, stirring for 2 minutes, until thickened.
11. Serve the sauce over the pork.

Skirt steak with Orange-Herb Pistou

Prep time: 10 minutes | Cook time: 20 minutes | Serves 4

- 1 pound skirt steak
- 8 tablespoons extra-virgin olive oil, divided
- 2 teaspoons salt, divided
- 1 teaspoon freshly ground black pepper, divided
- ½ cup chopped fresh flat-leaf Italian parsley
- ¼ cup chopped fresh mint leaves
- 2 garlic cloves, roughly chopped
- Zest and juice of 1 orange or 2 clementines
- 1 teaspoon red pepper flakes (optional)
- 1 tablespoon red wine vinegar

1. Heat the grill to medium-high heat or, if using an oven, preheat to 200 .
2. Rub the steak with 2 tablespoons olive oil and sprinkle with 1 teaspoon salt and ½ teaspoon pepper. Let sit at room temperature while you make the pistou.
3. In a food processor, combine the parsley, mint, garlic, orange zest and juice, remaining 1 teaspoon salt, red pepper flakes (if using), and remaining ½ teaspoon pepper.
4. Pulse until finely chopped. With the processor running, stream in the red wine vinegar and remaining 6 tablespoons olive oil until well combined.
5. This pistou will be more oil-based than traditional basil pesto.
6. Cook the steak on the grill, 6 to 8 minutes per side.
7. Remove from the grill and allow to rest for 10 minutes on a cutting board.
8. If cooking in the oven, heat a large oven-safe frying pan (cast iron works great) over high heat.
9. Add the steak and sear, 1 to 2 minutes per side, until browned.
10. Transfer the frying pan to the oven and cook 10 to 12 minutes, or until the steak reaches your desired temperature.
11. To serve, rasher the steak and drizzle with the pistou.

One-Pan Creamy Italian Bangers Orecchiette

Prep time: 5 minutes | Cook time: 25 minutes | Serves 2

- 1 tablespoon olive oil
- ½ medium onion, diced
- 2 garlic cloves, minced
- 2 ounces baby bella (cremini) mushrooms, rasherd
- 4 ounces hot or sweet Italian bangers
- ½ teaspoon Italian herb seasoning
- 1½ cups dry orecchiette pasta (about 6 ounces)
- 2 cups low-sodium chicken stock
- 2 cups packed baby spinach
- ¼ cup heavy cream
- Salt

1. Heat the olive oil in a sauté pan over medium-high heat.
2. Add the onion, garlic, and mushrooms and sauté for 5 minutes.
3. Remove the bangers from its casing and add it to the pan, breaking it up well.
4. Cook for another 5 minutes, or until the bangers is no longer pink.
5. Add the Italian herb seasoning, pasta, and chicken stock. Bring the mixture to a boil.
6. Cover the pan, reduce the heat to medium-low, and let it simmer for 10 to 15 minutes, or until the pasta is cooked. Remove from the heat.
7. Add the spinach and stir it in to let it wilt.
8. Add the cream and season with salt. The sauce will tighten up as it cools.
9. If it seems too thick, add additional chicken stock or water.

Stuffed Pork Loin with Sun-Dried Tomato and Goat Cheese

Prep time: 15 minutes | Cook time: 30 to 40 minutes | Serves 6

- 1 to 1½ pounds pork fillet
- 1 cup crumbled goat cheese
- 4 ounces frozen spinach, thawed and well drained
- 2 tablespoons chopped sun-dried tomatoes
- 2 tablespoons extra-virgin olive oil (or seasoned oil marinade from sun-dried tomatoes), plus ¼ cup, divided
- ½ teaspoon salt
- ½ teaspoon freshly ground black pepper
- Courgette Noodles or sautéed greens, for serving

1. Preheat the oven to 170. Cut cooking twine into eight (6-inch) pieces.
2. Cut the pork fillet in half lengthwise, leaving about an inch border, being careful to not cut all the way through to the other side.
3. Open the fillet like a book to form a large rectangle.
4. Place it between two pieces of greaseproof paper or cling film and pound to about ¼-inch thickness with a meat mallet, rolling pin, or the back of a heavy spoon.
5. In a small bowl, combine the goat cheese, spinach, sun-dried tomatoes, 2 tablespoons olive oil, salt, and pepper and mix to incorporate well.
6. Spread the filling over the surface of the pork, leaving a 1-inch border from one long edge and both short edges.
7. To roll, start from the long edge with filling and roll towards the opposite edge.
8. Tie cooking twine around the pork to secure it closed, evenly spacing each of the eight pieces of twine along the length of the roll.
9. In a Dutch oven or large oven-safe frying pan, heat ¼ cup olive oil over medium-high heat.
10. Add the pork and brown on all sides. Remove from the heat, cover, and bake until the pork is cooked through, 45 to 75 minutes, depending on the thickness of the pork.
11. Remove from the oven and let rest for 10 minutes at room temperature.
12. To serve, remove the twine and discard.
13. Rasher the pork into medallions and serve over Courgette Noodles or sautéed greens, spooning the cooking oil and any bits of filling that fell out during cooking over top.

Pork Fillet With Chermoula Sauce

Prep time: 15 minutes | Cook time: 20 minutes | Serves 2

- ½ cup fresh parsley
- ½ cup fresh coriander, fresh
- 6 small garlic cloves
- 3 tablespoons olive oil, divided
- 3 tablespoons freshly squeezed lemon juice
- 1 teaspoon smoked paprika
- 2 teaspoons cumin
- ½ teaspoon salt, divided
- Pinch freshly ground black pepper
- 1 (8-ounce) pork fillet

1. Preheat the oven to 215 and set the rack to the middle position.
2. In the bowl of a food processor, combine the parsley, coriander, fresh, garlic, 2 tablespoons of olive oil, the lemon juice, paprika, cumin, and ¼ teaspoon of salt.
3. Pulse 15 to 20 times, or until the mixture is fairly smooth.
4. Scrape the sides down as needed to incorporate all of the ingredients.
5. Transfer the sauce to a small bowl and set aside.
6. Season the pork fillet on all sides with the remaining ¼ teaspoon of salt and a generous pinch of pepper.
7. Heat the remaining 1 tablespoon of olive oil in a sauté pan.
8. Add the pork and sear for 3 minutes, turning often, until it's golden on all sides.
9. Transfer the pork to an oven-safe baking dish and roast for 15 minutes, or until the internal temperature registers 70.

Grilled Filet Mignon With Red Wine Mushroom Sauce

Prep time: 20 minutes | Cook time: 20 minutes | Serves 2

- 2 (3-ounce) pieces filet mignon
- 2 tablespoons olive oil, divided
- 8 ounces baby bella (cremini) mushrooms, quartered
- 1 large shallot, minced (about ⅓ cup)
- 2 teaspoons flour
- 2 teaspoons tomato paste
- ½ cup red wine
- 1 cup low-sodium chicken stock
- ½ teaspoon dried thyme
- 1 sprig fresh rosemary
- 1 teaspoon herbes de Provence
- ¼ teaspoon salt
- ¼ teaspoon garlic powder
- ¼ teaspoon onion powder
- Pinch freshly ground black pepper

1. Preheat the oven to 215 and set the oven rack to the middle position.
2. Remove the filets from the refrigerator about 30 minutes before you're ready to cook them.
3. Pat them dry with a paper towel and let them rest while you prepare the mushroom sauce.
4. In a sauté pan, heat 1 tablespoon of olive oil over medium-high heat.
5. Add the mushrooms and shallot and sauté for 10 minutes.
6. Add the flour and tomato paste and cook for another 30 seconds.
7. Add the wine and scrape up any browned bits from the sauté pan.
8. Add the chicken stock, thyme, and rosemary.
9. Stir the sauce so the flour doesn't form lumps and bring it to a boil.
10. Once the sauce thickens, reduce the heat to the lowest setting and cover the pan to keep the sauce warm.
11. In a small bowl, combine the herbes de Provence, salt, garlic powder, onion powder, and pepper.
12. Rub the beef with the remaining 1 tablespoon of olive oil and season it on both sides with the herb mixture.
13. Heat an oven-safe sauté pan over medium-high heat.
14. Add the beef and sear for 2½ minutes on each side.
15. Then, transfer the pan to the oven for 5 more minutes to finish cooking.
16. Use a meat thermometer to check the internal temperature and remove it at 65 for medium-rare.
17. Tent the meat with foil and let it rest for 5 minutes before serving topped with the mushroom sauce.

Greek-Style Braised Pork with Leeks

Prep time: 5 minutes | Cook time: 10 minutes | Serves 4 to 6

- 2 pounds boneless pork butt roast, trimmed and cut into 1-inch pieces
- Salt and pepper
- 3 tablespoons extra-virgin olive oil
- 2 pounds leeks, white and light green parts only, halved lengthwise, rasherd 1 inch thick, and washed thoroughly
- 2 garlic cloves, minced
- 1 (14.5-ounce) can diced tomatoes
- 1 cup dry white wine
- ½ cup chicken broth
- 1 bay leaf
- 2 teaspoons chopped fresh oregano

1. Adjust oven rack to lower-middle position and heat oven to 175 .
2. Pat pork dry with paper towels and season with salt and pepper.
3. Heat 1 tablespoon oil in Dutch oven over medium-high heat until just smoking.
4. Brown half of pork on all sides, about 8 minutes; transfer to bowl.
5. Repeat with 1 tablespoon oil and remaining pork; transfer to bowl.
6. Add remaining 1 tablespoon oil, leeks, ½ teaspoon salt, and ½ teaspoon pepper to fat left in pot and cook over medium heat, stirring occasionally, until softened and lightly browned, 5 to 7 minutes.
7. Stir in garlic and cook until fragrant, about 30 seconds.
8. Stir in tomatoes and their juice, scraping up any browned bits, and cook until tomato liquid is nearly evaporated, 10 to 12 minutes.
9. Stir in wine, broth, bay leaf, and pork with any accumulated juices and bring to simmer.
10. Cover, transfer pot to oven, and cook until pork is tender and falls apart when prodded with fork, 1 to 1½ hours.
11. Discard bay leaf. Stir in oregano and season with salt and pepper to taste.
12. Serve.

Chapter 8
Fish and Seafood

Prawn & Clam Paella
Prep time: 5 minutes|Cook time:25 minutes|Serves 4

- 2 tbsp olive oil
- 1 onion, chopped
- 4 garlic cloves, minced
- ½ cup dry white wine
- 2 cups bomba (Spanish) rice
- 4 cups chicken stock
- 1½ tsp sweet paprika
- 1 tsp turmeric powder
- ½ tsp freshly ground black pepper
- ½ tsp salt
- 1 pound small clams, scrubbed
- 1 pound fresh prawns, peeled and deveined
- 1 red bell pepper, diced
- 1 lemon, cut in wedges

1. Stir-fry onion and garlic in a tbsp. of oil on Sauté mode for 3 minutes.
2. Pour in wine to deglaze, scraping the bottom of the pot of any brown.
3. Cook for 2 minutes, until the wine is reduced by half.
4. Add in rice and water. Season with the paprika, turmeric, salt, and pepper.
5. Seal the lid and cook on High Pressure for 10 minutes. Do a quick release.
6. Remove to a plate and wipe the pot clean.
7. Heat the remaining oil on Sauté. Cook clams and prawns for 6 minutes, until the clams have opened and the Prawn are pink.
8. Discard unopened clams.
9. Arrange seafood and lemon wedges over paella, to serve.

Haddock Fillets with Crushed Potatoes
Prep time: 5 minutes|Cook time:20 minutes|Serves 4

- 8 ounces beer
- 2 eggs
- 1 cup flour
- ½ tbsp cayenne powder
- 1 tbsp cumin powder
- Salt and pepper to taste
- 4 haddock fillets
- Nonstick cooking spray
- 4 potatoes, cut into ¼- to ½-inch matchsticks
- 2 tbsp olive oil

1. In a bowl, whisk beer and eggs. In another bowl, combine flour, cayenne, cumin, black pepper, and salt.
2. Coat each fish piece in the egg mixture, then dredge in the flour mixture, coating all sides well.
3. Spray a baking dish with nonstick cooking spray.
4. Place in the fish fillets, pour ¼ cup of water and grease with cooking spray.
5. Place the potatoes in the pot and cover with water and place a trivet over the potatoes.
6. Lay the baking dish on top and seal the lid. Cook on High Pressure for 15 minutes. Do a quick release.
7. Drain and crush the potatoes with olive oil and serve with the fish.

Seafood Spicy Penne
Prep time: 5 minutes|Cook time:15 minutes|Serves 4

- 1 tbsp olive oil
- 1 onion, diced
- 16 ounces penne
- 24 ounces Arrabbiata sauce
- 3 cups chicken broth
- ½ tsp freshly ground black pepper
- ½ tsp salt
- 16 ounces scallops
- ¼ cup parmesan cheese, grated
- Basil leaves for garnish

1. Heat oil on Sauté and stir-fry onion for 5 minutes.
2. Stir in penne, arrabbiata sauce, and 2 cups of broth. Season with the black pepper and.
3. Seal the lid and cook for 6 minutes on High Pressure.
4. Do a quick release. Remove to a plate. Pour the remaining broth and add scallops.
5. Stir to coat, seal the lid and cook on High Pressure for 4 minutes.
6. Do a quick release.
7. Mix in the pasta and serve topped with parmesan cheese and basil leaves

Prawn Farfalle with Spinach
Prep time: 5 minutes|Cook time:15 minutes|Serves 4

- 1¼ pounds Prawn, peeled and deveined
- 1½ tsp salt
- 1 tbsp melted butter
- 2 garlic cloves, minced
- ¼ cup white wine
- 10 ounces farfalle
- 2½ cups water
- ⅓ cup tomato puree
- ½ tsp red Chili con carne flakes or to taste
- 1 tsp grated lemon zest
- 1 tbsp lemon juice
- 6 cups spinach

1. On Sauté, pour white wine, bring to simmer for 2 minutes to reduce the liquid by half.
2. Stir in the farfalle, water, salt, garlic, puréed tomato, Prawn, melted butter, and Chili con carne flakes. Seal the lid.
3. Cook for 5 minutes on High pressure.
4. Do a quick release.
5. Stir in lemon zest, juice, and spinach until wilted and soft.

Mussel Chowder with Oyster Water biscuits

Prep time: 5 minutes|Cook time:15 minutes|Serves 4

- 2 cups low carb oyster Water biscuits
- 2 tbsp olive oil
- ¼ cup finely grated Pecorino Romano cheese
- ½ tsp garlic powder
- Salt and pepper to taste
- 2 pancetta rashers
- 2 celery stalks, chopped
- 1 medium onion, chopped
- 1 tbsp flour
- ¼ cup white wine
- 1 cup water
- 20 ounces Tinned mussels, drained, liquid reserved
- 1 pound potatoes, peeled and cut chunks
- 1 tsp dried rosemary
- 1 bay leaf
- 1½ cups heavy cream
- 2 tbsp chopped fresh chervil

1. Fry pancetta on Sauté for 5 minutes, until crispy.
2. Remove to a paper towel-lined plate and set aside.
3. Sauté the celery and onion in the same fat for 1 minute, stirring, until the vegetables soften.
4. Mix in the flour to coat the vegetables.
5. Pour in the wine simmer. Cook for about 1 minute or until reduced by about one-third.
6. Pour in the water, the reserved mussel liquid, potatoes, salt, rosemary, and bay leaf.
7. Seal the lid and cook on High Pressure for 4 minutes.
8. Do a natural pressure release for 5 minutes.
9. Stir in the mussels and heavy cream. Press Sauté and bring the soup to a simmer to heat the mussels through.
10. Discard the bay leaf.
11. Spoon the soup into bowls and crumble the pancetta over the top.
12. Garnish with the chervil and Water biscuits, on side.

Baked Swordfish with Herbs

Prep time: 10 minutes|Cook time:20 minutes|Serves 4

- Olive oil spray
- 1 cup fresh Italian parsley
- ¼ cup fresh thyme
- ¼ cup lemon juice
- 2 cloves garlic
- ¼ cup extra-virgin olive oil
- ½ teaspoon salt
- 4 swordfish steaks (each 5 to 7 ounces)

1. Preheat the oven to 220 . Coat a large baking dish with olive oil spray.
2. In a food processor, pulse the parsley, thyme, lemon juice, garlic, olive oil, and salt 10 times.
3. Place the swordfish in the prepared baking dish.
4. Spoon the parsley mixture over the steaks.
5. Put the fish in the oven to bake for 17 to 20 minutes.

Garlic Rosemary Prawns

Prep time: 5 minutes|Cook time:10 minutes|Serves 2

- Melted butter: 1/2 tbsp.
- Green capsicum: rashers
- Eight prawns
- Rosemary leaves
- Salt & freshly ground black pepper
- 3-4 cloves of minced garlic

1. Mix all the ingredients in a bowl and marinate the prawns for at least 60 minutes.
2. Add two prawns and two rashers of capsicum to each skewer.
3. Let the Air Fryer preheat to 135 .
4. Cook for 5-6 minutes. Then set the temperature to 200 and cook for another minute.
5. Serve with lemon wedges.

Air-Fried Crumbed Fish

Prep time: 10 minutes|Cook time:12 minutes|Serves 4

- Four fish fillets
- Olive oil: 4 tablespoons
- One egg beaten
- Whole wheat breadcrumbs: ¼ cup

1. Preheat the Air Fryer to 165 .
2. In a bowl, mix well breadcrumbs with oil.
3. First, coat the fish in the egg mix (egg mix with water) and then in the breadcrumb mix. Coat well.
4. Place in the Air Fryer, and let it cook for 12 minutes.

Parmesan Garlic Crusted Salmon

Prep time: 5 minutes|Cook time:15 minutes|Serves 2

- Whole wheat breadcrumbs: 1/4 cup
- 4 cups of salmon
- Butter melted: 2 tablespoons
- ¼ tsp of freshly ground black pepper
- Parmesan cheese: 1/4 cup (grated)
- Minced garlic: 2 teaspoons
- Half teaspoon of Italian seasoning

1. Let the Air Fryer preheat to 200 , and spray the oil over the Air Fryer basket.
2. Pat dry the salmon.
3. In a bowl, mix Parmesan cheese, Italian seasoning, and breadcrumbs.
4. Mix melted butter with garlic in another bowl and add to the breadcrumbs mix. Mix well.
5. Add salt and ground black pepper to the salmon.
6. On top of every salmon piece, add the crust mix and press gently.
7. Add salmon to the Air Fryer and cook until done to your liking.

Sicilian Kale and Tunny Bowl

Prep time: 5 minutes|Cook time:15 minutes|Serves 6

- 1 pound kale, chopped, center ribs removed (about 12 cups)
- 3 tablespoons extra-virgin olive oil
- 1 cup chopped onion (about ½ medium onion)
- 3 garlic cloves, minced (about 1½ teaspoons)
- 1 (2.25-ounce) can rasherd olives, drained (about ½ cup)
- ¼ cup capers
- ¼ teaspoon crushed red pepper
- 2 teaspoons sugar
- 2 (6-ounce) cans tunny in olive oil, undrained
- 1 (15-ounce) can cannellini beans or great northern beans, drained and rinsed
- ¼ teaspoon freshly ground black pepper
- ¼ teaspoon kosher or sea salt

1. Fill a large stockpot three-quarters full of water, and bring to a boil.
2. Add the kale and cook for 2 minutes. (This is to make the kale less bitter.) Drain the kale in a colander and set aside.
3. Set the empty pot back on the stove over medium heat, and pour in the oil.
4. Add the onion and cook for 4 minutes, stirring often.
5. Add the garlic and cook for 1 minute, stirring often.
6. Add the olives, capers, and crushed red pepper, and cook for 1 minute, stirring often.
7. Add the partially cooked kale and sugar, stirring until the kale is completely coated with oil.
8. Cover the pot and cook for 8 minutes.
9. Remove the kale from the heat, mix in the tunny, beans, pepper, and salt, and serve.

Mediterranean Cod Stew

Prep time: 10 minutes|Cook time:20 minutes|Serves 6

- 2 tablespoons extra-virgin olive oil
- 2 cups chopped onion (about 1 medium onion)
- 2 garlic cloves, minced (about 1 teaspoon)
- ¾ teaspoon smoked paprika
- 1 (14.5-ounce) can diced tomatoes, undrained
- 1 (12-ounce) jar roasted red peppers, drained and chopped
- 1 cup rasherd olives, green or black
- ⅓ cup dry red wine
- ¼ teaspoon freshly ground black pepper
- ¼ teaspoon kosher or sea salt
- 1½ pounds cod fillets, cut into 1-inch pieces
- 3 cups rasherd mushrooms (about 8 ounces)

1. In a large stockpot over medium heat, heat the oil.
2. Add the onion and cook for 4 minutes, stirring occasionally.
3. Add the garlic and smoked paprika and cook for 1 minute, stirring often.
4. Mix in the tomatoes with their juices, roasted peppers, olives, wine, pepper, and salt, and turn the heat up to medium-high.
5. Bring to a boil. Add the cod and mushrooms, and reduce the heat to medium.
6. Cover and cook for about 10 minutes, stirring a few times, until the cod is cooked through and flakes easily, and serve.

Grilled Sea Bass with Tahini Sauce
Prep time: 10 minutes|Cook time:10 minutes|Serves 6

- 2 pounds sea bass
- Extra-virgin olive oil
- 1 cup tahini paste
- 1 tablespoon garlic, minced
- 1 teaspoon salt
- ⅓ cup lemon juice
- 1 cup water

1. Preheat a grill, grill pan, or lightly oiled frying pan to medium-high heat.
2. To prepare the sea bass, pat it dry with a paper towel and brush both sides with olive oil.
3. You can also use olive oil spray to save time.
4. In a small bowl, whisk together the tahini, garlic, salt, and lemon juice.
5. This will become very thick. Slowly add the water (about 1 cup) until you get to your desired consistency.
6. Place the sea bass on the grill or frying pan; do not move it for 6 minutes.
7. Flip the seabass over using a spatula and cook for another 7 minutes.
8. Put the sea bass onto a plate, and drizzle with the tahini sauce.
9. Serve with extra sauce on the side.

Spicy Trout over Sautéed Mediterranean Salad
Prep time: 10 minutes|Cook time:30 minutes|Serves 4

- 2 pounds rainbow trout fillets (about 6 fillets)
- Salt
- Ground white pepper
- 1 tablespoon extra-virgin olive oil
- 1 pound asparagus
- 4 medium golden potatoes, thinly rasherd
- 1 Spring onion, thinly rasherd, green and white parts separated
- 1 garlic clove, finely minced
- 1 large carrot, thinly rasherd
- 2 Roma tomatoes, chopped
- 8 pitted kalamata olives, chopped
- ¼ cup ground cumin
- 2 tablespoons dried parsley
- 2 tablespoons paprika
- 1 tablespoon vegetable bouillon seasoning
- ½ cup dry white wine

1. Lightly season the fish with salt and white pepper and set aside.
2. In a large sauté pan or frying pan, heat the oil over medium heat.
3. Add and stir in the asparagus, potatoes, the white part of the spring onions, and garlic to the hot oil.
4. Cook and stir for 5 minutes, until fragrant.
5. Add the carrot, tomatoes, and olives; continue to cook for 5 to 7 minutes, until the carrots are slightly tender.
6. Sprinkle the cumin, parsley, paprika, and vegetable bouillon seasoning over the pan.
7. Season with salt.
8. Stir to incorporate. Put the trout on top of the vegetables and add the wine to cover the vegetables.
9. Reduce the heat to low, cover, and cook for 5 to 7 minutes, until the fish flakes easily with a fork and juices run clear.
10. Top with Spring onion greens and serve.

Rosemary and Lemon Roasted Branzino

Prep time: 15 minutes|Cook time:30 minutes|Serves 2

- 4 tablespoons extra-virgin olive oil, divided
- 2 (8-ounce) branzino fillets, preferably at least 1 inch thick
- 1 garlic clove, minced
- 1 bunch spring onions, white part only, thinly rasherd
- ½ cup rasherd pitted kalamata or other good-quality black olives
- 1 large carrot, cut into ¼-inch rounds
- 10 to 12 small cherry tomatoes, halved
- ½ cup dry white wine
- 2 tablespoons paprika
- 2 teaspoons flaked salt
- ½ tablespoon ground Chili con carne pepper, preferably Turkish or Aleppo
- 2 rosemary sprigs or 1 tablespoon dried rosemary
- 1 small lemon, very thinly rasherd

1. Warm a large, oven-safe sauté pan or frying pan over high heat until hot, about 2 minutes.
2. Carefully add 1 tablespoon of olive oil and heat until it shimmers, 10 to 15 seconds.
3. Brown the branzino fillets for 2 minutes, skin-side up.
4. Carefully flip the fillets skin-side down and cook for another 2 minutes, until browned. Set aside.
5. Swirl 2 tablespoons of olive oil around the frying pan to coat evenly.
6. Add the garlic, spring onions, kalamata olives, carrot, and tomatoes, and let the vegetables sauté for 5 minutes, until softened.
7. Add the wine, stirring until all ingredients are well integrated. Carefully place the fish over the sauce.
8. Preheat the oven to 225 .
9. While the oven is heating, brush the fillets with 1 tablespoon of olive oil and season with paprika, salt, and Chili con carne pepper.
10. Top each fillet with a rosemary sprig and several rashers of lemon. Scatter the olives over fish and around the pan.
11. Roast until lemon rashers are browned or singed, about 10 minutes.

Tunny Slow-Cooked in Olive Oil

Prep time: 5 minutes|Cook time:45 minutes|Serves 4

- 1 cup extra-virgin olive oil, plus more if needed
- 4 (3- to 4-inch) sprigs fresh rosemary
- 8 (3- to 4-inch) sprigs fresh thyme
- 2 large garlic cloves, thinly rasherd
- 2 (2-inch) strips lemon zest
- 1 teaspoon salt
- ½ teaspoon freshly ground black pepper
- 1 pound fresh tunny steaks (about 1 inch thick)

1. Select a thick pot just large enough to fit the tunny in a single layer on the bottom.
2. The larger the pot, the more olive oil you will need to use.
3. Combine the olive oil, rosemary, thyme, garlic, lemon zest, salt, and pepper over medium-low heat and cook until warm and fragrant, 20 to 25 minutes, lowering the heat if it begins to smoke.
4. Remove from the heat and allow to cool for 25 to 30 minutes, until warm but not hot.
5. Add the tunny to the bottom of the pan, adding additional oil if needed so that tunny is fully submerged, and return to medium-low heat. Cook for 5 to 10 minutes, or until the oil heats back up and is warm and fragrant but not smoking.
6. Lower the heat if it gets too hot.
7. Remove the pot from the heat and let the tunny cook in warm oil 4 to 5 minutes, to your desired level of doneness.
8. For a tunny that is rare in the center, cook for 2 to 3 minutes.
9. Remove from the oil and serve warm, drizzling 2 to 3 tablespoons seasoned oil over the tunny.
10. To store for later use, remove the tunny from the oil and place in a container with a lid. Allow tunny and oil to cool separately.
11. When both have cooled, remove the herb stems with a slotted spoon and pour the cooking oil over the tunny.
12. Cover and store in the refrigerator for up to 1 week. Bring to room temperature to allow the oil to liquify before serving.

Prawn Ceviche Salad

Prep time: 15 minutes|Cook time: 2 hours|Serves 4

- 1 pound fresh Prawn, peeled and deveined
- 1 small red or yellow bell pepper, cut into ½-inch chunks
- ½ English cucumber, peeled and cut into ½-inch chunks
- ½ small red onion, cut into thin slivers
- ¼ cup chopped fresh coriander, fresh or flat-leaf Italian parsley
- ⅓ cup freshly squeezed lime juice
- 2 tablespoons freshly squeezed lemon juice
- 2 tablespoons freshly squeezed clementine juice or orange juice
- ½ cup extra-virgin olive oil
- 1 teaspoon salt
- ½ teaspoon freshly ground black pepper
- 2 ripe avocados, peeled, pitted, and cut into ½-inch chunks

1. Cut the Prawn in half lengthwise. In a large glass bowl, combine the Prawn, bell pepper, cucumber, onion, and coriander, fresh.
2. In a small bowl, whisk together the lime, lemon, and clementine juices, olive oil, salt, and pepper.
3. Pour the mixture over the Prawn and veggies and toss to coat.
4. Cover and refrigerate for at least 2 hours, or up to 8 hours.
5. Give the mixture a toss every 30 minutes for the first 2 hours to make sure all the Prawn "cook" in the juices.
6. Add the cut avocado just before serving and toss to combine.

Lemon-Pepper Trout

Prep time: 5 minutes|Cook time: 15 minutes|Serves 4

- 4 trout fillets
- 2 tablespoons olive oil
- ½ teaspoon salt
- 1 teaspoon black pepper
- 2 garlic cloves, rasherd
- 1 lemon, rasherd, plus additional wedges for serving

1. Preheat the air fryer to 190 .
2. Brush each fillet with olive oil on both sides and season with salt and pepper. Place the fillets in an even layer in the air fryer basket.
3. Place the rasherd garlic over the tops of the trout fillets, then top the garlic with lemon rashers and cook for 12 to 15 minutes, or until it has reached an internal temperature of 70 .
4. Serve with fresh lemon wedges.

Chapter 9
Vegetarian Recipes

Rocket Pizza
Prep time: 5 minutes|Cook time:15 minutes|Serves 4

- 1 pizza crust
- ½ cup tomato paste
- ¼ cup water
- 1 tsp sugar
- 1 tsp dried oregano
- 4 oz button mushrooms, chopped
- ½ cup grated gouda cheese
- 2 tbsp extra virgin olive oil
- 12 Olives
- 1 cup rocket for serving

1. Grease the bottom of a baking dish with one tablespoon of olive oil.
2. Line some greaseproof paper. Flour the working surface and roll out the pizza dough to the approximate size of your instant pot.
3. Gently fit the dough in the previously prepared baking dish.
4. In a bowl, combine tomato paste, water, sugar, and dry oregano.
5. Spread the mixture over dough, make a layer with button mushrooms and grated gouda.
6. Add a trivet inside the pot and pour in 1 cup of water.
7. Seal the lid, and cook for 15 minutes on High Pressure.
8. Do a quick release. Remove the pizza from your pot using a greaseproof paper.
9. Sprinkle with the remaining olive oil and top with olives and rocket . Cut and serve.

Aubergine Lasagna
Prep time: 5 minutes|Cook time:30 minutes|Serves 4

- 1 large Aubergine, chopped
- 4 oz mozzarella, chopped
- 3 oz Mascarpone cheese, at room temperature
- 2 tomatoes, chopped
- ¼ cup olive oil
- 1 tsp salt
- ½ tsp freshly ground black pepper
- 1 tsp oregano, dried

1. Grease a baking dish with olive oil.
2. Rasher the Aubergine and make a layer in the dish. Cover with mozzarella and tomato rashers. Top with mascarpone cheese.
3. Repeat the process until you run out of ingredients.
4. Meanwhile, in a bowl, mix olive oil, salt, pepper, and dried oregano.
5. Pour the mixture over the lasagna, and add ½ cup of water.
6. In your inner pot, Pour 1 ½ cups of water and insert a trivet.
7. Lower the baking dish on the trivet, Seal the lid and cook on High Pressure for 4 minutes.
8. When ready, do a natural release, for 10 minutes.

Spinach and Leeks with Goat Cheese
Prep time: 5 minutes|Cook time:5 minutes|Serves 2

- 9 oz fresh spinach
- 2 leeks, chopped
- 2 red onions, chopped
- 2 garlic cloves, crushed
- ½ cup goat cheese
- 3 tbsp olive oil
- 1 tsp flaked salt

1. Grease the inner pot with oil. Stir-fry leek, garlic, and onions, for about 5 minutes, on Sauté mode.
2. Add spinach and give it a good stir.
3. Season with salt and cook for 3 more minutes, stirring constantly.
4. Press Cancel, Transfer to a serving dish and sprinkle with goat's cheese.
5. Serve right away.

Colorful Vegetable Medley
Prep time: 5 minutes|Cook time:10 minutes|Serves 4

- 1 cup water
- 1 small head broccoli, broken into florets
- 16 asparagus, trimmed
- 1 small head cauliflower, broken into florets
- 5 ounces French beans
- 2 carrots, peeled and cut on bias
- Salt to taste

1. Add water and set trivet on top of water and place steamer basket on top.
2. In an even layer, spread French beans, broccoli, cauliflower, asparagus, and carrots in a steamer basket.
3. Seal the lid and cook on Steam for 3 minutes on High.
4. Release the pressure quickly.
5. Remove basket from the pot and season with salt.

Roasted Brussels Sprouts with Orange and Garlic
Prep time: 5 minutes|Cook time:10 minutes|Serves 4

- 1 pound Brussels sprouts, quartered
- 2 garlic cloves, minced
- 2 tablespoons olive oil
- ½ teaspoon salt
- 1 orange, cut into rings

1. Preheat the air fryer to 180 .
2. In a large bowl, toss the quartered Brussels sprouts with the garlic, olive oil, and salt until well coated.
3. Pour the Brussels sprouts into the air fryer, lay the orange rashers on top of them, and roast for 10 minutes.
4. Remove from the air fryer and set the orange rashers aside. Toss the Brussels sprouts before serving.

Sweet Chickpea & Mushroom Stew
Prep time: 5 minutes | Cook time: 15 minutes | Serves 4

- 1 cup chickpeas, cooked
- 1 onion, peeled, chopped
- A handful of French beans, trimmed
- 1 apple, cut into 1-inch cubes
- ½ cup sultanas
- 4 cherry tomatoes
- A handful of fresh mint
- 1 tsp grated ginger
- ½ cup freshly squeezed orange juice
- ½ tsp salt

1. Place all ingredients in the instant pot.
2. Pour enough water to cover. Cook on High Pressure for 8 minutes.
3. Do a natural release, for 10 minutes.

Asparagus and Prosciutto
Prep time: 5 minutes | Cook time: 5 minutes | Serves 4

- Eight ounces prosciutto rashers
- Eight asparagus spears, trimmed
- A pinch of salt and black pepper

1. Wrap the asparagus in prosciutto rashers and then season with salt and pepper.
2. Put all in your Air Fryer's basket and cook at 400° F for five minutes.

Balsamic Cabbage
Prep time: 5 minutes | Cook time: 8 minutes | Serves 4

- 1 red cabbage head, shredded
- 1 carrot, grated
- 1 tbsp. extra-virgin olive oil
- Salt and pepper
- ¼ cup balsamic vinegar

1. Place all ingredients in a pan that fits your Air Fryer, and stir well.
2. Put the pan in the Air Fryer and cook at 190 for eight minutes.

Citrus Asparagus with Pistachios
Prep time: 10 minutes | Cook time: 15 minutes | Serves 4

- 5 tablespoons extra-virgin olive oil, divided
- Zest and juice of 2 clementines or 1 orange (about ¼ cup juice and 1 tablespoon zest)
- ¼ teaspoon freshly ground black pepper
- ½ cup shelled pistachios
- 1 pound fresh asparagus
- 1 tablespoon water

1. In a small bowl, whisk together 4 tablespoons olive oil, the clementine and lemon juices and zests, vinegar, ½ teaspoon salt, and pepper. Set aside.
2. In a medium dry frying pan, toast the pistachios over medium-high heat until lightly browned, 2 to 3 minutes, being careful not to let them burn.
3. Transfer to a cutting board and coarsely chop. Set aside.
4. Trim the rough ends off the asparagus, usually the last 1 to 2 inches of each spear.
5. In a frying pan, heat the remaining 1 tablespoon olive oil over medium-high heat.
6. Add the asparagus and sauté for 2 to 3 minutes.
7. Sprinkle with the remaining ½ teaspoon salt and add the water.
8. Reduce the heat to medium-low, cover, and cook until tender, another 2 to 4 minutes, depending on the thickness of the spears.
9. Transfer the cooked asparagus to a serving dish.
10. Add the pistachios to the dressing and whisk to combine.
11. Pour the dressing over the warm asparagus and toss to coat.

Gorgonzola Sweet Potato Burgers
Prep time: 10 minutes | Cook time: 15 minutes | Serves 4

- 1 large sweet potato (about 8 ounces)
- 2 tablespoons extra-virgin olive oil, divided
- 1 cup chopped onion (about ½ medium onion)
- 1 cup old-fashioned rolled oats
- 1 large egg
- 1 tablespoon balsamic vinegar
- 1 tablespoon dried oregano
- 1 garlic clove
- ¼ teaspoon kosher or sea salt
- ½ cup crumbled Gorgonzola or blue cheese (about 2 ounces)
- Salad greens or 4 whole-wheat rolls, for serving (optional)

1. Using a fork, pierce the sweet potato all over and microwave on high for 4 to 5 minutes, until tender in the center.
2. Cool slightly, then rasher in half.
3. While the sweet potato is cooking, in a large frying pan over medium-high heat, heat 1 tablespoon of oil.
4. Add the onion and cook for 5 minutes, stirring occasionally.
5. Using a spoon, carefully scoop the sweet potato flesh out of the skin and put the flesh in a food processor.
6. Add the onion, oats, egg, vinegar, oregano, garlic, and salt. Process until smooth. Add the cheese and pulse four times to barely combine.
7. With your hands, form the mixture into four (½-cup-size) burgers. Place the burgers on a plate, and press to flatten each to about ¾-inch thick.
8. Wipe out the frying pan with a paper towel, then heat the remaining 1 tablespoon of oil over medium-high heat until very hot, about 2 minutes.
9. Add the burgers to the hot oil, then turn the heat down to medium.
10. Cook the burgers for 5 minutes, flip with a spatula, then cook an additional 5 minutes.
11. Enjoy as is or serve on salad greens or whole-wheat rolls.

Courgette-Aubergine Gratin

Prep time: 10 minutes | Cook time: 20 minutes | Serves 6

- 1 large Aubergine, finely chopped (about 5 cups)
- 2 large Courgette, finely chopped (about 3¾ cups)
- ¼ teaspoon freshly ground black pepper
- ¼ teaspoon kosher or sea salt
- 3 tablespoons extra-virgin olive oil, divided
- 1 tablespoon plain flour
- ¾ cup 2% milk
- ⅓ cup plus 2 tablespoons grated Parmesan cheese, divided
- 1 cup chopped tomato (about 1 large tomato)
- 1 cup diced or shredded fresh mozzarella (about 4 ounces)
- ¼ cup fresh basil leaves

1. Preheat the oven to 225.
2. In a large bowl, toss together the Aubergine, Courgette, pepper, and salt.
3. In a large frying pan over medium-high heat, heat 1 tablespoon of oil.
4. Add half the veggie mixture to the frying pan. Stir a few times, then cover and cook for 5 minutes, stirring occasionally.
5. Pour the cooked veggies into a baking dish. Place the frying pan back on the heat, add 1 tablespoon of oil, and repeat with the remaining veggies.
6. Add the veggies to the baking dish.
7. While the vegetables are cooking, heat the milk in the microwave for 1 minute. Set aside.
8. Place a medium saucepan over medium heat.
9. Add the remaining tablespoon of oil and flour, and whisk together for about 1 minute, until well blended.
10. Slowly pour the warm milk into the oil mixture, whisking the entire time.
11. Continue to whisk frequently until the mixture thickens a bit.
12. Add ⅓ cup of Parmesan cheese, and whisk until melted.
13. Pour the cheese sauce over the vegetables in the baking dish and mix well.
14. Gently mix in the tomatoes and mozzarella cheese.
15. Roast in the oven for 10 minutes, or until the gratin is almost set and not runny.
16. Garnish with the fresh basil leaves and the remaining 2 tablespoons of Parmesan cheese before serving.

Roasted Cauliflower and Tomatoes

Prep time: 5 minutes | Cook time: 25 minutes | Serves 4

- 4 cups cauliflower, cut into 1-inch pieces
- 6 tablespoons extra-virgin olive oil, divided
- 1 teaspoon salt, divided
- 4 cups cherry tomatoes
- ½ teaspoon freshly ground black pepper
- ½ cup grated Parmesan cheese

1. Preheat the oven to 225.
2. Add the cauliflower, 3 tablespoons of olive oil, and ½ teaspoon of salt to a large bowl and toss to evenly coat.
3. Pour onto a baking tray and spread the cauliflower out in an even layer.
4. In another large bowl, add the tomatoes, remaining 3 tablespoons of olive oil, and ½ teaspoon of salt, and toss to coat evenly. Pour onto a different baking tray.
5. Put the sheet of cauliflower and the sheet of tomatoes in the oven to roast for 17 to 20 minutes until the cauliflower is lightly browned and tomatoes are plump.
6. Using a spatula, spoon the cauliflower into a serving dish, and top with tomatoes, black pepper, and Parmesan cheese.
7. Serve warm.

Roasted Acorn Squash

Prep time: 10 minutes | Cook time: 35 minutes | Serves 6

- 2 acorn squash, medium to large
- 2 tablespoons extra-virgin olive oil
- 1 teaspoon salt, plus more for seasoning
- 5 tablespoons unsalted butter
- ¼ cup chopped sage leaves
- 2 tablespoons fresh thyme leaves
- ½ teaspoon freshly ground black pepper

1. Preheat the oven to 200.
2. Cut the acorn squash in half lengthwise.
3. Scrape out the seeds with a spoon and cut it horizontally into ¾-inch-thick rashers.
4. In a large bowl, drizzle the squash with the olive oil, sprinkle with salt, and toss together to coat.
5. Lay the acorn squash flat on a baking tray.
6. Put the baking tray in the oven and bake the squash for 20 minutes.
7. Flip squash over with a spatula and bake for another 15 minutes.
8. Melt the butter in a medium saucepan over medium heat.
9. Add the sage and thyme to the melted butter and let them cook for 30 seconds.
10. Transfer the cooked squash rashers to a plate. Spoon the butter/herb mixture over the squash.
11. Season with salt and black pepper.
12. Serve warm.

Quick Vegetable Kebabs
Prep time: 15 minutes|Cook time:15 minutes|Serves 4

- 4 medium red onions, peeled and rasherd into 6 wedges
- 4 medium Courgette, cut into 1-inch-thick rashers
- 4 capsicums, cut into 2-inch squares
- 2 yellow capsicums, cut into 2-inch squares
- 2 orange capsicums, cut into 2-inch squares
- 2 beefsteak tomatoes, cut into quarters
- 3 tablespoons Herbed Oil

1. Preheat the oven or grill to medium-high or 170 .
2. Thread 1 piece red onion, Courgette, different colored capsicums, and tomatoes onto a skewer.
3. Repeat until the skewer is full of vegetables, up to 2 inches away from the skewer end, and continue until all skewers are complete.
4. Put the skewers on a baking tray and cook in the oven for 10 minutes or grill for 5 minutes on each side.
5. The vegetables will be done with they reach your desired crunch or softness.
6. Remove the skewers from heat and drizzle with Herbed Oil.

Tortellini in Red Pepper Sauce
Prep time: 15 minutes|Cook time:10 minutes|Serves 4

- 1 (16-ounce) container fresh cheese tortellini (usually green and white pasta)
- 1 (16-ounce) jar roasted red peppers, drained
- 1 teaspoon garlic powder
- ¼ cup tahini
- 1 tablespoon red pepper oil (optional)

1. Bring a large pot of water to a boil and cook the tortellini according to package directions.
2. In a blender, combine the red peppers with the garlic powder and process until smooth.
3. Once blended, add the tahini until the sauce is thickened.
4. If the sauce gets too thick, add up to 1 tablespoon red pepper oil (if using).
5. Once tortellini are cooked, drain and leave pasta in colander.
6. Add the sauce to the bottom of the empty pot and heat for 2 minutes.
7. Then, add the tortellini back into the pot and cook for 2 more minutes. Serve and enjoy!

Moroccan Vegetable Tagine
Prep time: 20 minutes|Cook time:1 hours|Serves 6

- ½ cup extra-virgin olive oil
- 2 medium yellow onions, rasherd
- 6 celery stalks, rasherd into ¼-inch crescents
- 6 garlic cloves, minced
- 1 teaspoon ground cumin
- 1 teaspoon ginger powder
- 1 teaspoon salt
- ½ teaspoon paprika
- ½ teaspoon ground cinnamon
- ¼ teaspoon freshly ground black pepper
- 2 cups vegetable stock
- 1 medium Aubergine, cut into 1-inch cubes
- 2 medium Courgette, cut into ½-inch-thick semicircles
- 2 cups cauliflower florets
- 1 (13.75-ounce) can artichoke hearts, drained and quartered
- 1 cup halved and pitted green olives
- ½ cup chopped fresh flat-leaf parsley, for garnish
- ½ cup chopped fresh coriander, fresh leaves, for garnish
- Greek yogurt, for garnish (optional)

1. In a large, thick soup pot or Dutch oven, heat the olive oil over medium-high heat.
2. Add the onion and celery and sauté until softened, 6 to 8 minutes.
3. Add the garlic, cumin, ginger, salt, paprika, cinnamon, and pepper and sauté for another 2 minutes.
4. Add the stock and bring to a boil.
5. Reduce the heat to low and add the Aubergine, Courgette, and cauliflower.
6. Simmer on low heat, covered, until the vegetables are tender, 30 to 35 minutes.
7. Add the artichoke hearts and olives, cover, and simmer for another 15 minutes.
8. Serve garnished with parsley, coriander, fresh, and Greek yogurt (if using).

Parmesan and Herb Sweet Potatoes
Prep time: 10 minutes|Cook time:18 minutes|Serves 4

- 2 large sweet potatoes, peeled and cubed
- ¼ cup olive oil
- 1 teaspoon dried rosemary
- ½ teaspoon salt
- 2 tablespoons shredded Parmesan

1. Preheat the air fryer to 180 .
2. In a large bowl, toss the sweet potatoes with the olive oil, rosemary, and salt.
3. Pour the potatoes into the air fryer basket and roast for 10 minutes, then stir the potatoes and sprinkle the Parmesan over the top.
4. Continue roasting for 8 minutes more.
5. Serve hot and enjoy.

Chapter 10
Desserts

Honey Crema Catalana
Prep time: 5 minutes | Cook time: 10 minutes | Serves 4

- 5 cups heavy cream
- 8 egg yolks
- 1 cup honey
- 4 tbsp sugar
- 1 tsp cinnamon
- 1 vanilla extract
- ¼ tsp salt
- 1 cup water

1. In a bowl, combine heavy cream, egg yolks, vanilla, cinnamon, and honey.
2. Beat well with an electric mixer. Pour the mixture into 4 ramekins. Set aside.
3. Pour water in the pot and insert the trivet. Lower the ramekins on top.
4. Seal the lid, and cook for 10 minutes on High Pressure.
5. Do a quick pressure release.
6. Remove the ramekins from the pot and add a tablespoon of sugar in each ramekin.
7. Burn evenly with a culinary torch until brown.
8. Chill well and serve.

Marble Cherry Cake
Prep time: 5 minutes | Cook time: 25 minutes | Serves 6

- 1 cup flour
- 1½ tsp baking powder
- 1 tbsp powdered stevia
- ½ tsp salt
- 1 tsp cherry extract
- 3 tbsp butter, softened
- 3 eggs
- ¼ cup cocoa powder
- ¼ cup heavy cream

1. Combine all dry ingredients, except cocoa in a bowl.
2. Mix well to combine and add eggs, one at the time.
3. Beat well with a dough hook attachment for one minute.
4. Add sour cream, butter, and cherry extract.
5. Continue to beat for 3 more minutes.
6. Divide the mixture in half and add cocoa powder in one-half of the mixture. Pour the light batter into a greased baking dish.
7. Drizzle with cocoa dough to create a nice marble pattern.
8. Pour in one cup of water and insert the trivet. Lower the baking dish on top.
9. Seal the lid and cook for 20 minutes on High Pressure.
10. Release the pressure naturally, for about 10 minutes. Let it cool for a while and transfer to a serving plate.

Simple Apricot Dessert
Prep time: 5 minutes | Cook time: 35 minutes | Serves 8

- 2 lb fresh apricots, rinsed, drained
- 1 lb sugar
- 2 tbsp lemon zest
- 1 tsp ground nutmeg
- 10 cups water

1. Add apricots, sugar, water, nutmeg, and lemon zest.
2. Cook, stirring occasionally, until half of the water evaporates, on Sauté.
3. Press Cancel, and transfer the apricots and the remaining liquid into glass jars.
4. Let cool and close the lids.
5. Refrigerate overnight before use.

Dried Fruit Compote
Prep time: 5 minutes | Cook time: 10 minutes | Serves 6

- 4 cups water
- 3 tablespoons honey
- 2 (2-inch) strips lemon zest plus 1 tablespoon juice
- 2 cinnamon sticks
- 1¼ teaspoons ground coriander
- 2 cups (12 ounces) dried Turkish or Calimyrna figs, stemmed
- ¾ cup dried apricots
- ½ cup dried cherries

1. Bring water, honey, lemon zest and juice, cinnamon sticks, and coriander to boil in large saucepan over medium-high heat and cook, stirring occasionally, until honey has dissolved, about 2 minutes.
2. Stir in figs and apricots and return to boil.
3. Reduce heat to medium-low and simmer, stirring occasionally, until fruit is plump and tender, about 30 minutes.
4. Stir in cherries and cook until cherries are plump and tender, figs are just beginning to break apart, and liquid is thickened and syrupy, 15 to 20 minutes. Off heat, discard lemon zest and cinnamon sticks and let mixture cool slightly.
5. Serve warm, at room temperature, or chilled.

Stewed Plums with Almond Flakes
Prep time: 5 minutes | Cook time: 15 minutes | Serves 10

- 6 lb sweet ripe plums, pits removed and halved
- 2 cups white sugar
- 1 cup almonds, flaked

1. Drizzle the plums with sugar. Toss to coat.
2. Let it stand for about 1 hour to allow plums to soak up the sugar.
3. Transfer the plum mixture to the instant pot and pour 1 cup of water.
4. Seal the lid and cook on High Pressure for 30 minutes.
5. Allow the Pressure to release naturally, for 10 minutes.
6. Serve topped with almond flakes.

Turkish Stuffed Apricots with Rose Water and Pistachios
Prep time: 5 minutes | Cook time: 10 minutes | Serves 6

- ½ cup plain Greek yogurt
- ¼ cup sugar
- ½ teaspoon rose water
- ½ teaspoon grated lemon zest plus 1 tablespoon juice
- Salt
- 2 cups water
- 4 green cardamom pods, cracked
- 2 bay leaves
- 24 whole dried apricots
- ¼ cup shelled pistachios, toasted and chopped fine

1. Combine yogurt, 1 teaspoon sugar, rose water, lemon zest, and pinch salt in small bowl.
2. Refrigerate filling until ready to use.
3. Bring water, cardamom pods, bay leaves, lemon juice, and remaining sugar to simmer in small saucepan over medium-low heat and cook, stirring occasionally, until sugar has dissolved, about 2 minutes.
4. Stir in apricots, return to simmer, and cook, stirring occasionally, until plump and tender, 25 to 30 minutes. Using slotted spoon, transfer apricots to plate and let cool to room temperature.
5. Discard cardamom pods and bay leaves.
6. Bring syrup to boil over high heat and cook, stirring occasionally, until thickened and measures about 3 tablespoons, 4 to 6 minutes; let cool to room temperature.
7. Place pistachios in shallow dish.
8. Place filling in small zipper-lock bag and snip off 1 corner to create ½-inch opening.
9. Pipe filling evenly into opening of each apricot and dip exposed filling into pistachios; transfer to serving platter.
10. Drizzle apricots with syrup and serve.

Pomegranate-Quinoa Dark Chocolate Bark
Prep time: 10 minutes | Cook time: 10 minutes | Serves 6

- Nonstick cooking spray
- ½ cup uncooked tricolor or regular quinoa
- ½ teaspoon kosher or sea salt
- 8 ounces dark chocolate or 1 cup dark chocolate chips
- ½ cup fresh pomegranate seeds

1. In a medium saucepan coated with nonstick cooking spray over medium heat, toast the uncooked quinoa for 2 to 3 minutes, stirring frequently.
2. Do not let the quinoa burn. Remove the pan from the stove, and mix in the salt.
3. Set aside 2 tablespoons of the toasted quinoa to use for the topping.
4. Break the chocolate into large pieces, and put it in a gallon-size zip-top plastic bag.
5. Using a metal ladle or a meat pounder, pound the chocolate until broken into smaller pieces. (If using chocolate chips, you can skip this step.) Dump the chocolate out of the bag into a medium, microwave-safe bowl and heat for 1 minute on high in the microwave.
6. Stir until the chocolate is completely melted. Mix the toasted quinoa (except the topping you set aside) into the melted chocolate.
7. Line a large, rimmed baking tray with greaseproof paper. Pour the chocolate mixture onto the sheet and spread it evenly until the entire pan is covered.
8. Sprinkle the remaining 2 tablespoons of quinoa and the pomegranate seeds on top.
9. Using a spatula or the back of a spoon, press the quinoa and the pomegranate seeds into the chocolate.
10. Freeze the mixture for 10 to 15 minutes, or until set.
11. Remove the bark from the freezer, and break it into about 2-inch jagged pieces.
12. Store in a sealed container or zip-top plastic bag in the refrigerator until ready to serve.

Mini Mixed Berry Crumbles
Prep time: 15 minutes | Cook time: 30 minutes | Serves 2

- 1½ cups frozen mixed berries, thawed
- 1 tablespoon butter, softened
- 1 tablespoon brown sugar
- ¼ cup pecans
- ¼ cup oats

1. Preheat the oven to 170 and set the rack to the middle position.
2. Divide the berries between 2 (8-ounce) ramekins.
3. In a food processor, combine the butter, brown sugar, pecans, and oats, and pulse a few times, until the mixture resembles damp sand.
4. Divide the crumble topping over the berries.
5. Place the ramekins on a sheet pan and bake for 30 minutes, or until the top is golden and the berries are bubbling.

Crunchy Sesame Scones

Prep time: 10 minutes | Cook time: 15 minutes | Serves 14 to 16

- 1 cup sesame seeds, hulled
- 1 cup sugar
- 8 tablespoons (1 stick) salted butter, softened
- 2 large eggs
- 1¼ cups flour

1. Preheat the oven to 175. Toast the sesame seeds on a baking tray for 3 minutes. Set aside and let cool.
2. Using a mixer, cream together the sugar and butter.
3. Add the eggs one at a time until well-blended.
4. Add the flour and toasted sesame seeds and mix until well-blended.
5. Drop spoonfuls of Scone dough onto a baking tray and form them into round balls, about 1-inch in diameter, similar to a walnut.
6. Put in the oven and bake for 5 to 7 minutes or until golden brown.
7. Let the Scones cool and enjoy.

Almond Scones

Prep time: 5 minutes | Cook time: 10 minutes | Serves 4 to 6

- ½ cup sugar
- 8 tablespoons (1 stick) room temperature salted butter
- 1 large egg
- 1½ cups plain flour
- 1 cup ground almonds or almond flour

1. Preheat the oven to 185.
2. Using a mixer, cream together the sugar and butter.
3. Add the egg and mix until combined.
4. Alternately add the flour and ground almonds, ½ cup at a time, while the mixer is on slow.
5. Once everything is combined, line a baking tray with greaseproof paper.
6. Drop a tablespoon of dough on the baking tray, keeping the Scones at least 2 inches apart.
7. Put the baking tray in the oven and bake just until the Scones start to turn brown around the edges, about 5 to 7 minutes.

Citrus Pound Cake

Prep time: 10 minutes | Cook time: 45 minutes | Serves 8

FOR THE CAKE
- Nonstick cooking spray
- 1 cup sugar
- ⅓ cup extra-virgin olive oil
- 1 cup buttermilk
- 1 lemon, zested and juiced
- 2 cups plain flour
- 1 teaspoon bicarbonate of soda
- 1 teaspoon salt

FOR THE GLAZE
- 1 cup icing sugar
- 1 to 2 tablespoons freshly squeezed lemon juice
- ½ teaspoon vanilla extract

TO MAKE THE CAKE
1. Preheat the oven to 175. Line a 9-inch loaf pan with greaseproof paper and coat the paper with nonstick cooking spray.
2. In a large bowl, whisk together the sugar and olive oil until creamy. Whisk in the buttermilk and lemon juice and zest. Let it stand for 5 to 7 minutes.
3. In a medium bowl, combine the flour, bicarbonate of soda, and salt. Fold the dry ingredients into the buttermilk mixture and stir just until incorporated.
4. Pour the batter into the prepared pan and smooth the top. Bake until a toothpick or skewer inserted into the middle comes out clean with a few crumbs attached, about 45 minutes.
5. Remove the cake from the oven and cool for at least 10 minutes in the pan. Transfer to a cooling rack placed over a baking tray and cool completely.

TO MAKE THE GLAZE
1. In a small bowl, whisk together the icing sugar, lemon juice, and vanilla until smooth.
2. Pour the glaze over the cooled cake, allowing the excess to drip off the cake onto the baking tray beneath.

Individual Apple Pockets

Prep time: 5 minutes | Cook time: 15 minutes | Serves 6

- 1 organic puff pastry, rolled out, at room temperature
- 1 Gala apple, peeled and rasherd
- ¼ cup brown sugar
- ⅛ teaspoon ground cinnamon
- ⅛ teaspoon ground cardamom
- Nonstick cooking spray
- Honey, for topping

1. Preheat the oven to 175.
2. Cut the pastry dough into 4 even discs.
3. Peel and rasher the apple. In a small bowl, toss the rashers with brown sugar, cinnamon, and cardamom.
4. Spray a muffin tin very well with nonstick cooking spray.
5. Be sure to spray only the muffin holders you plan to use.
6. Once sprayed, line the bottom of the muffin tin with the dough and place 1 or 2 broken apple rashers on top.
7. Fold the remaining dough over the apple and drizzle with honey.
8. Bake for 15 minutes or until brown and bubbly.

Strawberry Panna Cotta

Prep time: 10 minutes, plus 6 hours | Cook time: 10 minutes | Serves 4

- 2 tablespoons warm water
- 2 teaspoons gelatin powder
- 2 cups heavy cream
- 1 cup rashered strawberries, plus more for garnish
- 1 to 2 tablespoons sugar-free sweetener of choice (optional)
- 1½ teaspoons pure vanilla extract
- 4 to 6 fresh mint leaves, for garnish (optional)

1. Pour the warm water into a small bowl. Sprinkle the gelatin over the water and stir well to dissolve. Allow the mixture to sit for 10 minutes.
2. In a liquidiser or a large bowl, if using an immersion blender, combine the cream, strawberries, sweetener (if using), and vanilla.
3. Blend until the mixture is smooth and the strawberries are well puréed.
4. Transfer the mixture to a saucepan and heat over medium-low heat until just below a simmer.
5. Remove from the heat and cool for 5 minutes.
6. Whisking constantly, add in the gelatin mixture until smooth.
7. Divide the custard between ramekins or small glass bowls, cover and refrigerate until set, 4 to 6 hours.
8. Serve chilled, garnishing with additional rashered strawberries or mint leaves (if using).

Chocolate Chia Pudding

Prep time: 10 minutes, plus 6 to 8 hours | Cook time: 10 minutes | Serves 4

- 2 cups heavy cream
- ¼ cup unsweetened cocoa powder
- 1 teaspoon almond extract or vanilla extract
- ½ or 1 teaspoon ground cinnamon
- ¼ teaspoon salt
- ½ cup chia seeds

1. In a saucepan, heat the heavy cream over medium-low heat to just below a simmer.
2. Remove from the heat and allow to cool slightly.
3. In a liquidiser or large bowl, if using an immersion blender, combine the warmed heavy cream, cocoa powder, almond extract, cinnamon, and salt and blend until the cocoa is well incorporated.
4. Stir in the chia seeds and let sit for 15 minutes.
5. Divide the mixture evenly between ramekins or small glass bowls and refrigerate at least 6 hours, or until set.
6. Serve chilled.

Olive Oil Cake

Prep time: 5 minutes | Cook time: 12 to 15 minutes | Serves 4

- Olive oil cooking spray
- 1½ cups wholemeal flour, plus more for dusting
- 3 eggs
- ⅓ cup honey
- ½ cup olive oil
- ½ cup unsweetened almond milk
- ½ teaspoon vanilla extract
- ½ teaspoon almond extract
- 1 teaspoon baking powder
- ½ teaspoon salt

1. Preheat the air fryer to 190.
2. Lightly coat the interior of an 8-by-8-inch baking dish with olive oil cooking spray and a dusting of wholemeal flour.
3. Knock out any excess flour.
4. In a large bowl, beat the eggs and honey until smooth.
5. Slowly mix in the olive oil, then the almond milk, and finally the vanilla and almond extracts until combined.
6. In a separate bowl, whisk together the flour, baking powder, and salt.
7. Slowly incorporate the dry ingredients into the wet ingredients with a rubber spatula until combined, making sure to scrape down the sides of the bowl as you mix.
8. Pour the batter into the prepared pan and place it in the air fryer.
9. Bake for 12 to 15 minutes, or until a toothpick inserted in the center comes out clean.

Grilled Fruit Kebabs With Honey Labneh

Prep time: 15 minutes | Cook time: 10 minutes | Serves 2

- ⅔ cup prepared labneh, or, if making your own, ⅔ cup full-fat plain Greek yogurt
- 2 tablespoons honey
- 1 teaspoon vanilla extract
- Pinch salt
- 3 cups fresh fruit cut into 2-inch chunks (pineapple, rockmelon, nectarines, strawberries, plums, or mango)

1. If making your own labneh, place a colander over a bowl and line it with cheesecloth.
2. Place the Greek yogurt in the cheesecloth and wrap it up.
3. Put the bowl in the refrigerator and let sit for at least 12 to 24 hours, until it's thick like soft cheese.
4. Mix honey, vanilla, and salt into labneh.
5. Stir well to combine and set it aside.
6. Heat the grill to medium (about 150) and oil the grill grate.
7. Alternatively, you can cook these on the stovetop in a heavy grill pan (cast iron works well).
8. Thread the fruit onto skewers and grill for 4 minutes on each side, or until fruit is softened and has grill marks on each side.
9. Serve the fruit with labneh to dip.

Appendix 1 Measurement Conversion Chart

Volume Equivalents (Dry)	
US STANDARD	METRIC (APPROXIMATE)
1/8 teaspoon	0.5 mL
1/4 teaspoon	1 mL
1/2 teaspoon	2 mL
3/4 teaspoon	4 mL
1 teaspoon	5 mL
1 tablespoon	15 mL
1/4 cup	59 mL
1/2 cup	118 mL
3/4 cup	177 mL
1 cup	235 mL
2 cups	475 mL
3 cups	700 mL
4 cups	1 L

Volume Equivalents (Liquid)		
US STANDARD	US STANDARD (OUNCES)	METRIC (APPROXIMATE)
2 tablespoons	1 fl.oz.	30 mL
1/4 cup	2 fl.oz.	60 mL
1/2 cup	4 fl.oz.	120 mL
1 cup	8 fl.oz.	240 mL
1 1/2 cup	12 fl.oz.	355 mL
2 cups or 1 pint	16 fl.oz.	475 mL
4 cups or 1 quart	32 fl.oz.	1 L
1 gallon	128 fl.oz.	4 L

Temperatures Equivalents	
FAHRENHEIT(F)	CELSIUS(C) APPROXIMATE)
225 °F	107 °C
250 °F	120 ° °C
275 °F	135 °C
300 °F	150 °C
325 °F	160 °C
350 °F	180 °C
375 °F	190 °C
400 °F	205 °C
425 °F	220 °C
450 °F	235 °C
475 °F	245 °C
500 °F	260 °C

Weight Equivalents	
US STANDARD	METRIC (APPROXIMATE)
1 ounce	28 g
2 ounces	57 g
5 ounces	142 g
10 ounces	284 g
15 ounces	425 g
16 ounces (1 pound)	455 g
1.5 pounds	680 g
2 pounds	907 g

Appendix 2 The Dirty Dozen and Clean Fifteen

The Environmental Working Group (EWG) is a nonprofit, nonpartisan organization dedicated to protecting human health and the environment Its mission is to empower people to live healthier lives in a healthier environment. This organization publishes an annual list of the twelve kinds of produce, in sequence, that have the highest amount of pesticide residue-the Dirty Dozen-as well as a list of the fifteen kinds of produce that have the least amount of pesticide residue-the Clean Fifteen.

THE DIRTY DOZEN	
The 2016 Dirty Dozen includes the following produce. These are considered among the year's most important produce to buy organic:	
Strawberries	Spinach
Apples	Tomatoes
Nectarines	Bell peppers
Peaches	Cherry tomatoes
Celery	Cucumbers
Grapes	Kale/collard greens
Cherries	Hot peppers
The Dirty Dozen list contains two additional items kale/collard greens and hot peppers-because they tend to contain trace levels of highly hazardous pesticides.	

THE CLEAN FIFTEEN	
The least critical to buy organically are the Clean Fifteen list. The following are on the 2016 list:	
Avocados	Papayas
Corn	Kiw
Pineapples	Eggplant
Cabbage	Honeydew
Sweet peas	Grapefruit
Onions	Cantaloupe
Asparagus	Cauliflower
Mangos	
Some of the sweet corn sold in the United States are made from genetically engineered (GE) seedstock. Buy organic varieties of these crops to avoid GE produce.	

Appendix 3 Index

A

all-purpose flour 50, 53
allspice 15
almond 5, 14
ancho chile 10
ancho chile powder 5
apple 9
apple cider vinegar 9
arugula 51
avocado 11

B

bacon 52
balsamic vinegar 7, 12, 52
basil 5, 8, 11, 13
beet 52
bell pepper 50, 51, 53
black beans 50, 51
broccoli 51, 52, 53
buns 52
butter 50

C

canola oil 50, 51, 52
carrot 52, 53
cauliflower 5, 52
cayenne 5, 52
cayenne pepper 52
Cheddar cheese 52
chicken 6
chili powder 50, 51
chipanle pepper 50
chives 5, 6, 52
cinnamon 15
coconut 6
Colby Jack cheese 51
coriander 52
corn 50, 51
corn kernels 50
cumin 5, 10, 15, 50, 51, 52

D

diced panatoes 50
Dijon mustard 7, 12, 13, 51
dry onion powder 52

E

egg 14, 50, 53
enchilada sauce 51

F

fennel seed 53
flour 50, 53
fresh chives 5, 6, 52
fresh cilantro 52
fresh cilantro leaves 52
fresh dill 5
fresh parsley 6, 52
fresh parsley leaves 52

G

garlic 5, 9, 10, 11, 13, 14, 50, 51, 52, 53
garlic powder 8, 9, 52, 53

H

half-and-half 50
hemp seeds 8
honey 9, 51

I

instant rice 51

K

kale 14
kale leaves 14
ketchup 53
kosher salt 5, 10, 15

L

lemon 5, 6, 14, 51, 53
lemon juice 6, 8, 11, 13, 14, 51
lime 9, 12
lime juice 9, 12
lime zest 9, 12

M

maple syrup 7, 12, 53
Marinara Sauce 5
micro greens 52
milk 5, 50
mixed berries 12
Mozzarella 50, 53
Mozzarella cheese 50, 53
mushroom 51, 52
mustard 51, 53
mustard powder 53

N

nutritional yeast 5

O

olive oil 5, 12, 13, 14, 50, 51, 52, 53
onion 5, 50, 51
onion powder 8
oregano 5, 8, 10, 50

P

panatoes 50, 52
paprika 5, 15, 52
Parmesan cheese 51, 53
parsley 6, 52
pesto 52
pink Himalayan salt 5, 7, 8, 11
pizza dough 50, 53
pizza sauce 50
plain coconut yogurt 6
plain Greek yogurt 5
porcini powder 53
potato 53

R

Ranch dressing 52
raw honey 9, 12, 13
red pepper flakes 5, 8, 14, 15, 51, 53
ricotta cheese 53

S

saffron 52
Serrano pepper 53
sugar 10
summer squash 51

T

tahini 5, 8, 9, 11
thyme 50
toasted almonds 14
tomato 5, 50, 52, 53
turmeric 15

U

unsalted butter 50
unsweetened almond milk 5

V

vegetable broth 50
vegetable stock 51

W

white wine 8, 11
wine vinegar 8, 10, 11

Y

yogurt 5, 6

Z

zucchini 50, 51, 52, 53

ELLA R. LOPEZ

Printed in Great Britain
by Amazon